Finding Home

Exploring God's Dream

in Our Neighborhoods

Julie Heiliger & Stephanie Wood

WITH BOB ADGATE AND ANDY HUNT

NavPress

A NavPress resource published in alliance
with Tyndale House Publishers

NavPress ⬮

NavPress is the publishing ministry of The Navigators, an international Christian organization and leader in personal spiritual development. NavPress is committed to helping people grow spiritually and enjoy lives of meaning and hope through personal and group resources that are biblically rooted, culturally relevant, and highly practical.

For more information, visit NavPress.com.

Finding Home: Exploring God's Dream in Our Neighborhoods

Copyright © 2019 by The Navigators. All rights reserved.

A NavPress resource published in alliance with Tyndale House Publishers

NAVPRESS and the NavPress logo are registered trademarks of NavPress, The Navigators, Colorado Springs, CO. *TYNDALE* is a registered trademark of Tyndale House Ministries. Absence of ® in connection with marks of NavPress or other parties does not indicate an absence of registration of those marks.

The Team:
David Zimmerman, Acquisitions Editor; Elizabeth Schroll, Copy Editor; Olivia Eldredge, Operations Manager; Eva Winters, Designer

Cover illustration of city copyright © mdyn/Adobe Stocks. All rights reserved.

Cover illustration of neighborhood copyright © bsd555/Adobe Stock. All rights reserved.

Cover photograph of watercolor background copyright © korkeng/Adobe Stock. All rights reserved.

Interior illustration of Europe map copyright © filo/iStockphoto. All rights reserved.

All Scripture quotations, unless otherwise indicated, are taken from the Holy Bible, *New International Version,*® *NIV.*® Copyright © 1973, 1978, 1984, 2011 by Biblica, Inc.® Used by permission. All rights reserved worldwide. Scripture quotations marked MSG are taken from *THE MESSAGE,* copyright © 1993, 2002, 2018 by Eugene H. Peterson. Used by permission of NavPress. All rights reserved. Represented by Tyndale House Publishers. Scripture quotations marked NASB are taken from the New American Standard Bible,® copyright © 1960, 1962, 1963, 1968, 1971, 1972, 1973, 1975, 1977, 1995 by The Lockman Foundation. Used by permission. Scripture quotations marked NLT are taken from the *Holy Bible,* New Living Translation, copyright © 1996, 2004, 2015 by Tyndale House Foundation. Used by permission of Tyndale House Publishers, Carol Stream, Illinois 60188. All rights reserved.

Some of the anecdotal illustrations in this book are true to life and are included with the permission of the persons involved. All other illustrations are composites of real situations, and any resemblance to people living or dead is purely coincidental.

For information about special discounts for bulk purchases, please contact Tyndale House Publishers at csresponse@tyndale.com, or call 1-855-277-9400.

ISBN 978-1-64158-401-2

Printed in the United States of America

26	25	24	23	22	21
7	6	5	4	3	2	1

Contents

Foreword

It was such a delightfully ridiculous proposition.

A few years back, a few colleagues and I were asked if we would consider framing discussions and walking alongside a few hundred followers of Jesus for a new venture focused on neighborhood presence within an international ministry.

All over the country, nearly everyone we met was curious, teachable, and committed to Christ and his Kingdom. Oh, and most had already raised resources to allow them to listen deeply to their neighbors and connect their neighbors' gifts, *and* they were committed to a life of prayer and presence. We almost couldn't believe it.

Most of the insights and grounded wisdom of this book rose from our shared learning over years of journeying together. We collectively began to trust the conviction that if you are a follower of Jesus and you want to change the world, there is no better place to begin than *right where you are*.

I can think of no greater call than to make disciples who join God in healing and transforming every single neighborhood on the planet. It's an audacious mission that is met with some serious challenges. So it's only fair that at the beginning you are given a fair warning.

You can't change the world—not really.

If it's God's dream we are truly after, then we need to trust that God is the hero of the story, not us. The transformation we seek is a gift to be received, not a technique to be mastered. If you are anything like me, this will take years of unlearning and relearning, and this book will help immensely.

You also can't go alone—at least, not really.

Although one-on-one relationships are vital, the most powerful form of discipleship is plural. The best showcase of the Good News of Jesus is when everyday people form teams around God's dream for that place. This book is loaded with practical and inspiring ideas to make and sustain life-giving relationships right where you are.

We all long for home, and we all long to tangibly see God's Kingdom in our everyday lives. If you commit to journey through this book, especially with others, I think you'll be astonished with the stories you get to tell in joining a God who says, "Behold, I am making all things new" (Revelation 21:5, NASB).

Tim Soerens
author of Everywhere You Look:
Discovering the Church Right Where You Are

Preface

I've spent more than thirty years as part of the worldwide disciplemaking movement known as The Navigators. We are really big on, well, making disciples. We want to make disciples who make more disciples. We desire that disciples of Jesus multiply all over the world.

That's what we do. That's the "what." But how about the "why"? Why do we want disciples of Jesus?

God has a dream. His dream is nothing less than the restoration, the reconciliation, and the renewal of all things. Genesis tells us that the original creation was perfect. Adam and Eve lived in harmony with their place, with one another, and with God himself. A temptation to be like God, a terrible choice, rebellion, sin, and brokenness shattered it all. Yet God's dream remains.

What was can be again. We know this deep down in our souls. We know that things can be better, that relationships can be healed, that people can fit together in harmony with God and with each other. This is the hope of the gospel.

Through the death, burial, and resurrection of Jesus, all things will be made whole again. This is the power of God—his Kingdom rule and reign—being unleashed. Where does this happen? Every day all over the world, as God's people pray that his Kingdom would come and his will would be done *on earth* as it is in heaven.

So why make disciples? Because we live in a fragmented and broken world. A committed community of Christ's disciples can bring hope and healing when they engage at the local level through the lens of God's Kingdom. I was recently talking about this with a few friends, committed disciple-makers who had recently transitioned to civilian life from our Navigators Military ministries and wanted help applying what they had learned in that context to this new one. I stressed the importance of faithful presence, of committed community, and of engaging with not only the people but also the place they live.

One of the guys expressed surprise. He said, "Al, I thought you would be banging the drum of discipleship, since almost no one else is doing so."

I responded that discipleship burns in my heart, but if the presence of the disciples of Jesus does not make a Kingdom impact on the places we live, what's the point?

Finding Home: Exploring God's Dream in Our Neighborhoods is designed to help you partner with others in the place you live for the flourishing of that place. It is full of stories by real-life practitioners. I've been to their neighborhoods, I've prayed with them, and I've dreamed with them about what it would be like for God's will to be done in their places. It's a movement that I hope you will join.

Al Engler
Disciplemakers for Life mission leader,
The Navigators

Introduction

Welcome home. We're really glad you're there—in your home, on your street, in your town. It's no accident; in fact, we think it is evidence. You being you, right where you are, is evidence that God is present and the Spirit is on the move, rustling through the streets and the schools and the shops and the hearts of the people in your neighborhood.

The collection of stories, reflections, and studies that you hold in your hand is our invitation to you to reimagine the very ordinary space you inhabit. It's an invitation to explore and experiment with the notion that, perhaps, your front porch and your kitchen table, the neighborhood playground and the corner store are more than what they first appear. We believe that when the Spirit of God ignites the hearts of the people of God with a passion for the places they live, these ordinary things become the formidable resources for gospel renewal. We're talking about the kind of gospel renewal that looks and smells and tastes and sounds and even feels like good news.

It's our dream that Christians would take their faith beyond the church building and would begin to follow Jesus into the neighborhood. We're certain that people will find he is already there and at work. "Thy kingdom come, thy will be done" (Matthew 6:10, KJV) is a prayer that calls for our participation, and it can begin right where we live.

May we humbly suggest that you gather a few followers of Jesus who live nearby? Spend the next ten weeks together working through this tool. Let's reimagine together what God might do in and through you if you partnered together in his name on behalf of the place you live. This conversation and journey is an exploration that will take you deeper into your own town. *Finding Home* is a ten-week tool exploring what it means to love our neighbors and our neighborhood. It's not a journey best taken by oneself. So these next weeks you will be reading, studying, and practicing—together with others.

This isn't exactly a Bible study, though we hope you will dig into Scripture. It's more of a Bible study meets supper club meets book club. We call it an invitation. It's an invitation to explore and experiment together with what it might be like to partner with other followers of Jesus on behalf of your place. During our time together, you will:

- study the scriptural basis for your calling to the place you live;
- develop practical tools to love people in your community; and

- discern whether to intentionally join with others locally to invest in the people and places that you call home.

Part 1 of this tool explores scriptural foundations for **Committed Communities** partnering together on behalf of their places. Committed Communities are what we call small groups of Christ-followers who reside in the same geographic area and are intentionally living life together in a way that edifies one another, cares for the lost and broken world around them, and seeks to know and glorify Jesus. These initial chapters will take us into the Bible.

In part 2, we will spend the remainder of our time experimenting with the practical matters of Committed Community life. These next weeks together are intended to be interactive. They are permission to wonder, explore, dream, and conspire together about what God might do if his people banded together for the sake of the neighborhood.

With much love,
Your co-conspirators:

Julie Heiliger and Stephanie Wood
with Bob Adgate and Andy Hunt

Glossary of Terms

As we journey together, you may find yourself learning terms that are new or unfamiliar. To make our voyage smoother and more enjoyable, it will be helpful for us to have a similar understanding of the concepts presented in *Finding Home*. We offer you this glossary as a quick reference. Terms marked in **bold type** at first mention in each chapter are defined for you here.

built space—The man-made elements of a community, such as roads, sidewalks, buildings, gardens, parks, etc.

calculated moments—The formal or planned moments that a Committed Community spends together on a regular basis.

casual moments—The informal or spontaneous moments that a Committed Community spends together on a regular basis.

Committed Community—A small group of Christ-followers who reside in the same geographic area and are intentionally living life together in a way that edifies one another, cares for the lost and broken world around them, and seeks to know and glorify Jesus.

faithful presence—Entering into your current circumstance with steadfastness and consistency while remaining responsive to both your limitations and responsibilities for relating to God, to others, and to the created world.

linking—The practice of growing meaningful relationships with people and places both inside and outside of your own parish.

living above place—The unconscious belief that one's experience of life is not interrelated and connected to the place one lives. This leads to a sense of disconnection, as if one's choices do not affect the environment, the built space, other people, and the land.

parish—"A unique word that recalls a geography large enough to live life together (live, work, play, and so forth) and small enough to be known as a character within it."[1] Interchangeable words in this tool include *neighborhood*, *place*, or *local community*.

People of Peace—Inspired by Jesus' sending of the apostles in Matthew 10 and Luke 10, People of Peace are non-Christians who nonetheless are receptive to Christians who enter their community and seek to make meaningful connections. They serve as connectors for Christians to other people and contexts, so that Christians have the opportunity to share and demonstrate the love of Christ.

third places—"Public places on neutral ground where people can gather and interact."[2] Third places level the playing field of social interaction, allowing for individuals and communities to strengthen ties and self-understanding. Coffee houses, pubs, and gyms are examples of third places.

Up/In/Out—The three-dimensional lifestyle that Jesus lived while on earth. *Up* alludes to Jesus' relationship with the Father, *In* to his chosen disciples, and *Out* to the broken world around him.

PART 1

The Foundations of Committed Community Life

Getting Started

Exploring Your Context

The Christian experience, from start to finish,
is a journey of faith.

WATCHMAN NEE, *Journeying Towards the Spiritual*

"If these walls could only talk" is an idiom that expresses our common human desire to know the history of a place. Our fascination with history museums belies the reality that artifacts are more than just old things. These physical objects, just like our towns and cities and neighborhoods, hold stories that connect us to the past and to each other.

As I (Stephanie) began to love the town I call home, I discovered there was much I did not know. A relative newcomer, I didn't know where the old hardware store used to be and that the now-vacant Daughtry building had once been a vibrant department store. More than that, I didn't know about the indigenous people who had once inhabited the land. I didn't know that before it was a bedroom community, my town had been full of orchards and chicken farms. I didn't know the racist history and the steps toward reconciliation. But I learned, and I am still learning.

On Your Own

When we know the stories of our hometowns, they become dearer to us. Our hometowns become ours as we know their past and weave our own lives into the stories of the future.

Knowing the story of the physical space you inhabit can provide important context to guide you in the journey ahead. This week, there is no Bible study; instead, consider spending thirty minutes researching your town's history. Google is an invaluable resource, but a local library or a longtime resident may provide you with colorful stories.

How to Use *Finding Home*

Before you get started, here are some practical notes about *Finding Home*:

It is important that one person (or up to two) fills the role of facilitator. This person should be the same throughout all ten weeks. The role of the facilitator is to help lead the group discussions as well as the weekly group activities. If your group has not already done this, please select a facilitator. (See appendix A for facilitator notes.)

Before diving into the meat of the material, it is important that the group gathers to connect, set expectations, and learn how to use the resource. Don't skip week one!

To prepare for weeks two through five, each individual should complete the reading and Bible study portions before gathering together as a group. The early weeks set a biblical foundation for discussion and practice to come. Sections to be completed individually are marked *On Your Own*, and they are the only prep that needs to be done beforehand. These *On Your Own* sections should take about thirty minutes of preparation before the group meeting.

During the weekly meeting time, groups will interact with questions marked "Group Discussion Questions" as well as complete the group activity listed for that particular week. These sections are marked *Time Together*.

Please note, part 2 has no Bible study. The only preparation to be completed before group time is the reading.

All activities throughout this resource are meant to be done in a group setting; they do not require advance preparation. All group activities should take anywhere from twenty to fifty minutes to complete, depending on the week.

Committed Community

Telling a New Story to a Culture Living above Place

*Living with air pollution increases your odds
of dying early by 5%. Living with obesity, 20%.
Excessive drinking, 30%. And living with loneliness?
It increases our odds of dying early by 45%.*

BRENÉ BROWN,
"America's Crisis of Disconnection Runs Deeper than Politics"

Our first week together, we spent some time getting to know one another and the stories of our cities, towns, and neighborhoods. It is our hope that the exercise of researching your community left you feeling curious and that as the weeks progress, you will become a student of the place where you live. This week we will explore the theme of relational connectedness in the particularity of place throughout Scripture. We will look at a story that demonstrates how when people partner together, **built space** can be transformed for community flourishing.

On Your Own

More than one hundred years ago, sociologist Georg Simmel observed that the mobility of a society disrupts connection and creates isolation. As people migrate (particularly to urban areas), they leave behind their social connections and struggle to connect again in their new places. In other words, Simmel's research suggests stable investment in the communities we live in helps us enjoy more connected and joy-filled lives. Georg Simmel could not have imagined how relevant his work has become in the last one hundred years. We drive and fly, text and use social media, but do we ever really connect? The unintended consequence of mobility is an exponential rise in loneliness. And science is bearing out this truth: Loneliness is terminal.

In *The New Parish: How Neighborhood Churches Are Transforming Mission, Discipleship, and Community*, Tim Soerens, Paul Sparks, and Dwight Friesen call this epidemic of loneliness **"living above place."** When we live above place, we no longer know the stories of our neighborhoods and towns. We don't know the shop owners. We don't know who grows our food or where it comes from. We lose a sense of gift economy wherein Aunt Sally trades hemming her neighbor's slacks for his cutting her grass. In crisis, we trade a fabric of real human care and connection for social services and public aid. This exchange costs us some of our humanity.

What if "living above place" is not just a social and

cultural problem? What if it is a spiritual problem? Loneliness and isolation might very well be the fallout of original sin. God's dream is that people would live deeply connected and restored lives; that dream was delayed and its expression marred when people first tried to live independently of their God. The invitation today is for believers to live together in relational wholeness that transforms both the individual and the community. We are invited to participate in God's dream for the restoration of the world.

Lisa Sharon Harper, in her book *The Very Good Gospel*, looks carefully at the language in the Creation narrative and uncovers some paradigm-shifting truth. Genesis 1:31 says, "God saw all that he had made, and it was *very good*" (emphasis added). The phrase "it was good" gets repeated over and over. It was good; God declared it so. To the Western mind, *good* has a particular meaning. "That steak was good!" or "That movie was good!" In these cases, goodness is inherent in the thing described. This is not the case in the Hebrew understanding. The "very good"-ness of creation was understood in relationship to the other created things. The evening is good in relation to morning. The water is good in relation to air. Plants and animals, earth and sky, humanity and deity, we all are wholly connected, and that connection is holy! The Hebrews knew this as shalom, which is to say God created all to be perfectly complete and perfectly connected, full of abundance and peace. The Good News of the gospel begins in Genesis and ends with Jesus restoring the connected goodness of the Garden.[1]

Christ-followers are invited to participate with Jesus in the "re-membering" of his good work. In fact, many of the world's longest-standing **Committed Communities**, from the early Desert Fathers to L'Arche communities of today, have come to see their function in the body of Christ as both a gospel witness and a sacred presence in the world. They see their relationships with God, each other, and their community as an alternate story to the epidemic loneliness of the culture. By their very existence, they proclaim there is another way to be. In addition to being a hope-filled alternative, Committed Community is a sacramental presence. A sacrament is an outward expression of an inward grace; it is a grace lived out. As communities practice the interconnected good-ness God intended, they become a picture of God's grace. Their presence and posture in their neighborhoods begin to weave back into place an interconnected fabric of love and belonging—they join with Jesus in his restoration work.

Followers of Jesus who are considering partnering on behalf of their communities naturally ask, "What should we do?" That is not a wrong question; it is just not the *first* question. First ask: "What shall we be?" As Jesus-followers partnering with Christ on behalf of their neighborhoods, Committed Communities will always be an alternate story of hope and grace, a juxtaposition to a lonely and isolated world.

Part 2 of this tool will unpack how Committed Communities go about being an alternate story of hope and grace. But for now, allow time to consider that we are, in fact, better together.

Bible Study

Nehemiah provides an early picture of Committed Community functioning as an alternative story of hope in a particular place. Much of the book is narrated in Nehemiah's own voice. Nehemiah was a Jewish man who was a high-ranking official in the court of the Persian king. At the time of the story, the Jewish people had returned to Jerusalem from years of exile. Upon returning home, they found their city in ruins. Read Nehemiah 1:1-4 for a first-person account of the circumstances in Jerusalem.

1. What were the physical conditions in Jerusalem?

   _____

   _____

   _____

2. The text says survivors were in "bad shape" (Nehemiah 1:3, MSG). Imagine you were in the shoes of Jerusalem's inhabitants. What do you suppose was the emotional landscape of the ruined city?

   _____

   _____

   _____

3. What was Nehemiah's response to the news about Jerusalem?

_____

_____

_____

_____

4. Read Nehemiah 2:1-5. What did Nehemiah ask of King Artaxerxes?

_____

Nehemiah's request was granted by the king, so he traveled to Jerusalem. Don't lose sight of the fact that God's plan for Nehemiah was to go and invest in a particular place. This is nearly universal in Scripture. God calls people to places. Upon arrival, Nehemiah addresses the survivors of the Exile. Read Nehemiah 2:17-18.

5. What circumstances did Nehemiah identify in his address to the people?

_____

_____

_____

_____

6. What did Nehemiah invite the survivors to participate in?

_____

_____

_____

7. How do you think the emotional landscape of Jerusalem changed after Nehemiah's invitation?

_____

8. Reread Nehemiah 2:18. We believe that this is the beginning of a Committed Community functioning as a new story of hope in Jerusalem. What were some key features of this budding Committed Community?

_____

_____

Nehemiah 3 identifies real people in the neighborhood who created a network of labor robust enough to rebuild. Go through the chapter and count how many people were named as involved in the project.

9. What do you think is the significance of this long list of names?

_____

_____

10. In chapter 4, we see the building community faced with opposition from their enemies and discouraged by the enormity of their task. Read Nehemiah 4:14-15. Nehemiah responded with encouragement to the tired and discouraged builders. What could Committed Communities today learn from his example?

_____

_____

11. Read Nehemiah 4:19-20. What was Nehemiah's response to builders being widely separated from each other?

_____

_____

12. How critical is proximity for neighbors to partner for the flourishing of their place?

_____

_____

13. What are some practices that could counteract disjointed community life?

_____

_____

_____

A Story: The Gospel Garden

My college degree is in horticulture, but my life path made me a professional photographer and took me to Chicago, San Francisco, then Oakland. I landed here in Castro Valley, California, bruised by new motherhood, isolation, and another round of depression. God gave my family not only a new home but a gift meant just for me: a garden. It had five raised beds surrounded by three-foot-tall weeds behind a much-needed deer fence. It was like precious gold to me.

I spent the winter poring over seed catalogs and dreaming of different veggie combinations and flowers. As I began to do the work, other women asked to join me in weeding. That winter I spent a lot of time with two women, Corie and Cathy. We talked mostly of the struggles of children and our marriages as we uprooted grass and nettles. I did over one hundred hours of weeding that first winter.

In the early spring, our missional community came out for a work day to mulch, plant seedlings, and wheelbarrow dirt into a large raised bed that my husband, Eric, helped add to the garden.

Then my friend Jenna came along. She has become my partner with this garden that has grown larger than myself. We've seeded, weeded, transplanted, and I've taught her how to collect seeds for the next season. We have spent countless hours over the last two years together on gardening. While our hands were engaged with dirt, we have wrestled with ideas of death, love, politics, identity, and the hurt she's endured from the mainstream church. She has flourished here. She has become more free, more herself—and she knows how to grow kale! She has settled into being a beloved member of our community and family.

The garden has also been a place to teach our children. My son Leif, who is now four, has been in this garden with me several times each week since he was two. His interest comes and goes, but he still makes his rounds every day to check for ripe zucchini, tomatoes, cucumbers, and pumpkins, and almost daily munches on mint leaves. Growing food is normal for him. Kids in our community have pulled onions, cut flowers, watched butterflies, and collected their favorite tomato, the Sungold. They've played with the garden hose and eaten fresh carrots. They have planted seeds and watered the herbs. I've had a teenager look at lettuce and proclaim, "That's it? You just pick it and eat it?"

God has used this garden to heal me. He has given me a physical space to feel at home, to feel my truest self. He has used my daily walks through our redwood-mulched paths to sustain me in my life season. It has been a place for others to work, to belong, to learn about their food and how to grow it. It is a haven for hummingbirds, honeybees, and a few farm cats. It has been a conversation starter with our new Russian friends and a show-and-tell for dinner parties. It has made partnerships, friendships, and bouquets of flowers for our tables. It's given food to our neighbors and made conversations between people with little in common. It's been quiet and safe. It has been a place of discipleship, of big questions and heartache.

This year our missional community helped build a new garden gate. We added three more large raised beds that are now filled with zinnia flowers and giant pumpkins that the seed packet claims will grow up to a hundred pounds. We have added a teenage neighbor, Emma, who is now a regular and is interested in botany for a career. She is eager to learn how to prune tomatoes, and I get to listen about prom and her classes.

The garden has no preference; it welcomes all. The loud and reckless two year old, the eager-to-learn teenager, the hardworking grandpa, and the tired mom. It has space for us all.

—Jessie, Castro Valley, California

Time Together

Group Discussion Questions
led by facilitator

1. Jessie's garden story is a story of her choosing to root into the actual land in a way that fostered the "very good-ness" of Kingdom relationships. In what ways are you connected to your neighborhood and community that express the divine "good-ness" of relationship?

2. Why should loneliness and "living above place" matter to the follower of Jesus?

3. How do we band together in a way that can offer hope and healing to the communities we live in?

4. How is personal transformation related to community life, civic engagement, education, and land stewardship?

Group Activity
led by facilitator

Secular scientists and sociologists are finding disturbing trends that are spiritually relevant. Read the article below together.

Google: "America's Crisis of Disconnection Runs Deeper than Politics" by Brené Brown.

The article states:

Terrorism is time-released fear. Its ultimate goal is to embed fear so deeply in the heart of a community that fear becomes a way of life. This unconscious way of living then fuels so much anger and blame that people start to turn on one another. Terrorism is most effective when we allow fear to take root in our culture. Then it's only a matter of time before we become fractured, isolated, and driven by our perceptions of scarcity.[2]

Now read Romans 12. It paints a picture of community life and partnership life that stands in stark contrast to a terrorized and lonely culture. Imagine how this different way of being might be played out on the streets and sidewalks of your place through a Committed Community. Do you see followers of Jesus in your place living this way already? Why or why not?

For additional study, consider these activities:

- Research local periodicals. Does local news provide examples of people living above place or, conversely, people building connections of love and care?

- Watch: "The Lethality of Loneliness: John Cacioppo at TEDxDesMoines," https://www.youtube.com/watch?v=_0hxl03JoA0.[3]

Why Place Matters

"In Christianity," we might say, "we have callings, *not* places.*"
And usually in those callings, or "vocations," we regard place as
irrelevant. By definition, callings "call" us somewhere else. So
rootedness is not a widely practiced Christian virtue. In fact it is
often not considered a virtue at all, but a spiritual impediment.
Pilgrimage is an important part of the Christian life, but it was
not what we were made for. We were made to make a particular
corner of creation our home: we were made for place.*

LOREN WILKINSON, foreword to *No Home Like Place*

Last week we were introduced to stories of everyday folks having an impact on their place. From ancient Hebrews rebuilding their city to a current-day garden story in California, we saw people partnering together to form flourishing communities. But the equation works both ways: The literal geography people inhabit also shapes and forms them. This week we will investigate why place matters.

On Your Own

In the 1800s, Mark Twain once joked, "In Boston they ask, How much does he know? in New York, How much is he worth? in Philadelphia, Who were his parents?"[1] Twain's quip calls out the values each American city held in high esteem. The remark highlights how where a person lives affects his or her worldview. After more than one hundred years, Twain's overarching insight stands the test of time.

Place can form the very essence of who we are. Without us even making a conscious decision about it, the communities where we live—and even the physical land that we dwell on—all shape us. How we view ourselves, each other, and God is molded, at least in part, by our physical surroundings and by the people who live near us.

Throughout the Bible, God reveals the significance that he puts on place. Perhaps two of the most compelling verses on this topic come from the book of Acts.

Read the following:

> From one man he made all the nations, that they should inhabit the whole earth; and he marked out their appointed times in history and the boundaries of their lands. God did this so that they would seek him and perhaps reach out for him and find him, though he is not far from any one of us.
>
> ACTS 17:26-27

- Put a box around *all the nations* and underline *inhabit* and *boundaries of their lands*.

- According to this passage, why did God appoint the times and the boundaries of every nation? Circle the three reasons given.

The Greek word used for *nations* in this passage is *ethnos*, which refers to people groups. Even though we read the word *nations* in our English versions, Luke, the author of Acts, would not have had geopolitical countries in mind (such as those we might think of today: Spain, India, Kenya, and so forth). Instead, Luke referred to people who were grouped together by a common language and culture. These are much smaller clusters of people than what today's geopolitical countries represent.

Here's why this is significant. Think about how strategic the placing of every people group is. Their existence in history and *the boundaries of their lands* (i.e., the places where they live) are all designed to help them seek, reach out for, and find God. Through God's design, place is inextricably linked to God's spiritual purposes for every ethnic community that has ever existed.

It should not surprise us that place and spiritual purpose are linked together. This is a theme that one can see throughout Scripture.

Bible Study

Before your group meets, choose at least two of the passages below to read on your own, and answer the corresponding questions.

GENESIS 1:26-28; 2:7-15

1. What charge did God give to the first man and woman (verse 1:28)?

_____

_____

_____

2. Where did God place them to live out this commission (verse 2:15)? Theorize for a moment why God may have given Adam and Eve these physical boundaries to live within even though the entire earth was unpopulated.

_____

_____

_____

GENESIS 28:10-22

3. Where did this biblical account take place (verse 19)?

_____

_____

4. What did God promise in verse 13?

_____

_____

5. What was God's main purpose in giving Jacob's descendants that land (verse 14)?

_____

_____

_____

JOHN 1:14-18

6. What place did Jesus leave, and what was his destination (verse 14)?

_____

_____

7. What was Jesus' relocation all about? (See also Romans 3:23-26.)

_____

_____

MARK 5:1-20

8. Where did the demon-possessed man live (verse 20)?

_____

_____

_____

9. The man requested to accompany Jesus, but what alternative did Jesus propose (verses 18-19)?

_____

_____

10. Why did Jesus deny the request (verse 19)?

_____

_____

_____

These passages illustrate just a few examples of how often God ties a person's calling to a specific place. Eden was the best place for Adam and Eve to subdue the earth and begin populating it. Bethel (and the surrounding area) was the best place for Jacob and his descendants to live so that they could bless all the families of the earth. Jesus needed to leave heaven and come to earth (Israel, specifically) in order to dispense grace and truth and explain the heavenly Father to his people. The formerly demon-possessed man needed to remain at home in the Decapolis[2] in order for the message of Jesus' mercy to go forth to his community.

We haven't even explored how Joseph's purpose was tied to Egypt, Ruth's to Bethlehem, Daniel's to Babylon, or Esther's to Susa, to name a few. Again and again, we see how God accomplishes his Kingdom work through people in the places where they settle.

Historically, land and place have held a status of importance around the world. But in our current Western culture, many don't take the time to pause, learn about, and consider the significance of their physical surroundings and local community. As followers of Christ, many of us do not even think to contemplate how living in our specific physical locations might actually be the strategic placement of God for his purposes. And we certainly don't find it natural to ponder how God may have placed a *group* of his disciples in a specific place for a reason. But what if? What if God wants to call his sons and daughters (even those from different local church bodies!) to unite in their place on behalf of his name? What if . . . ?

The boundaries within which the Lord places his people are purposeful. Where he has placed *you* is purposeful. God may not call you to plant roots and stay in your current location forever, but while you are there, he has you there for a reason, both for your sake and for the sake of the people around you.

May God grant joy to you and your neighboring brothers and sisters in Christ as you discover the significance of your place and his purpose for you in it.

Time Together

Group Discussion Questions
led by facilitator

1. Think about the community (or communities) that you lived in while growing up. How was your worldview

shaped as you experienced life in your neighborhood, attended local schools, interacted with the various ethnic groups in your community (or lack thereof), lived at your socioeconomic level, and so forth?

2. Acts 17:16-27 says that God has appointed each people group their time and place to live so that they might seek him and find him. Reflect on your own life. How has God used place to draw you to himself?

3. Once one becomes a child of God, it is that child's sacred role to be Christ's ambassador to the people around him or her (2 Corinthians 5:20). As such, Jesus' followers become one of the main ways that people can reach out and find him. What does this mean for you and your purpose in the place where you live?

4. All Christ-followers are called to share the gospel with others; however, one's purpose in his or her neighborhood and community is not limited to this. Take some time to pray and ask God what other specific purposes he may have for you in your place. In what ways might he want you to holistically represent him and his Kingdom in your community?

Group Activity
led by facilitator

Paul Sparks, Tim Soerens, and Dwight J. Friesen use the word ***parish*** to define place. According to them, *parish* is "a

A Story: From Exile to Home

*Frankly, I felt like a misfit in my neighborhood. Why? Because even after ten years in the same house, I was not well connected locally and didn't really want to be! You see, I began **living above place** as a child: We military "brats" learn early not to get attached to any place since we'll just be uprooted in two to three years, when our parents get new orders. Serving as a missionary for fifteen years in two African countries reinforced that childhood message. Love people, of course. But "sent ones" shouldn't get too attached to geography because they may never see their non-American friends again. When a family crisis brought me to the United States suddenly—prematurely—I stubbornly called Denver "Babylon" because I felt I was in forced exile. Not a very good mindset to learn to live in place!*

Ten years ago, my elderly mother came to live with me. So we selected a home in a retirees' neighborhood, more for her needs than for mine. After all, I'm still called to minister among the younger generation—not senior citizens. (Confession: I am a senior citizen!) And I have lots of dear friends all over the world. So who needs local friends? Being an introvert and single and traveling a lot didn't help.

Then Mom passed away.

God really got my attention a few months ago when I wanted to go to a concert but couldn't think of anyone local to invite along. While driving home alone that evening, I heard the Lord say, "Judy, if you're going to live in this town, it's time you started really living in this town!" Living intentionally in place suddenly made sense—even for me! God opened my eyes to look beyond my block to other places I frequent—or could begin frequenting.

Just in the last few months, I have:

- *begun quilting with Sue, a neighbor;*
- *joined a Sunday school class that meets over the Word and gathers socially two to three times a month;*

- *taken a walking tour of historical sites in my small town;*
- *gone to high tea with the local historical society;*
- *volunteered to serve at my HOA's pool-opening party;*
- *joined an aqua aerobics class at the rec center;*
- *visited a ladies bunco night sponsored by my HOA (okay, the game is super boring, but the women are diverse and interesting); and*
- *hosted a Fourth of July party on my deck, which overlooks the Front Range of the Rockies.*

I am excited to be trusting God to help me grow in really living in my place. Instead of viewing myself as an annual plant living for a while in a pot on the front porch, I yearn to experience being a shrub planted long-term in this amazing place where I live.

—Judy, Parker, Colorado

unique word that recalls a geography large enough to live life together (live, work, play, etc.) and small enough to be known as a character within it."[3]

Knowing the boundaries of your place can help to focus your prayer for your parish as well as clarify how and where you might be able to lean into the pulse of your community.

Take five to ten minutes now to individually draw out the boundaries of what you consider your personal parish to be. Here are some questions that Sparks, Soerens, and Friesen use to help people define their parish:

- Where is the center of your neighborhood?
- Where are there natural or man-made boundaries?
- Where are the parks, schools, major businesses, and other **third places** (examples: coffee shops, public libraries, and clubs)?

Share your sketches with one another. Note if any of your boundaries overlap. Then as a group, choose three to four of the following questions to answer and discuss:

- What types of people live in your parish?
  Think ethnicity, socioeconomic status, religious representation, age, major employers, and so forth.
- Where do people in your community go to connect? What do the places where they gather tell you about the people? What do these observations tell you about your place as a whole?

- Why do people like or dislike living in your community?
- What other Christ-followers do you know who live in your parish?
- What is the history of your place?
- Where is the Kingdom of God being expressed in your parish?
- Where is there brokenness in your community? Who is hurting the most?

Faithful Presence in the Parish

If there are benevolent consequences of our engagement
with the world . . . it is precisely because it is not rooted
in a desire to change the world for the better but
rather because it is an expression of a desire to
honor the creator of all goodness, beauty, and truth,
a manifestation of our loving obedience to God, and
a fulfillment of God's command to love our neighbor.

JAMES DAVISON HUNTER, *To Change the World*

Over the last couple of sessions, we have looked at how the people of God partnering together can contribute to flourishing community, and we've established that God puts people in their particular places for his purposes. People partnering together in the **parish** matters to God! But how we engage matters too. Many of us have good intentions when we seek to love our neighbors and our communities well. Yet good intentions are not enough. Our intentions and subsequent actions must continuously be shaped and led by the Spirit. This week we will explore the idea of **faithful presence** as a principle that can provide some guardrails to help us engage our places well.

On Your Own

From the beginning, God has chosen to be with mankind. In the Garden, God walked with Adam and Eve in the cool of the day. Many years later, God made his place with his people in the Tabernacle and then in the Temple. At the opening of the New Testament, Immanuel (literally, "God with us") is born and resides among his chosen people. And at the end of his life on earth, Immanuel promises to always be with his disciples. The presence of God is a sacred gift; the presence of God is our sacred example.

Committed Communities are not only a picture of the relational wholeness that God offers this world, and they are not only placed by the Lord in literal, physical boundaries—they are also deeply rooted and present within those borders.

This idea of being rooted and present can be summed up in the words *faithful presence*. Faithful presence can be defined as entering into your current circumstance (for our purposes, your parish) with steadfastness and consistency while remaining responsive to both your limitations and your responsibilities for relating to God, to others, and to the created world. In other words, it is a faithful relationship right where you live with God, others, and your place.

Steadfastness and Consistency

Like childhood best friends, a Committed Community will be loyal to its parish and the people in it. Likewise, a Committed Community will remain involved with its place regularly and over time. In a sense, the group becomes folded into the life of their neighborhood.[1]

Committed Communities do not feel the need to go somewhere else in order to have a vibrant ministry; rather, they live and minister among those with whom they share space. They make disciples as they go, even if that means simply walking next door or down the street to the local coffee shop or corner store. From the serious to the strange, the Mennonite to the Muslim, the homemaker to the homeless, the cyclist to the couch potato, the American to the Armenian, these followers of Jesus in the neighborhood live among the very people they long to see know the love of Christ.

But it is not simply enough to be among; what we are setting forth is the importance of being *faithfully* among. Faithfulness is essential because it implies commitment, engagement, relational connection, and love.

I (Julie) attended a small Bible college in the Washington, DC, area. To engage with my love of volleyball, I joined the campus team. Whether home or away, my parents came to almost every match my team played. All. Four. Years. There were moments when I felt my mom and dad's loyalty was possibly a bit much, especially since we weren't some high-performance team making waves in the world of sport. We were a small team playing in the circuit of other small Bible colleges. But these thoughts of mine quickly passed away.

Even when we traveled out of state and nobody else made the trip to support us, my parents were there in the stands cheering us on. They came to dinner with us after matches;

they brought baked goods for us to enjoy; they celebrated my fellow players' birthdays; they learned about the lives of the young women with whom I played. As my teammates saw my parents' dedication to them, they began to anticipate and appreciate my mom and dad's presence. Over time, relationships developed, and my teammates came to love my parents and my parents them. There was something special about knowing that someone was always in our corner, even if we were miles away from home.

My pastor, Dave Michener, says, "You can fake a lot of things, but you can't fake showing up." For a group of Christ-followers who are committed to loving their neighbors alongside each other, being faithfully present is paramount. Like my teammates coming to value and depend on the loyal cheerleading of my mom and dad, those in your parish will likely come to notice and appreciate your love and care for them and your place. But perhaps even more than this, your willingness to show up consistently and for the long haul will ignite a love in your heart for your neighbors and your community. And if a Christlike love serves as the foundation for all you do and say, Jesus will be seen and honored in your place.

The Importance of Faithful Presence

Faithful presence allows for followers of Christ to advance the *gospel* of Jesus. As immediate neighbors and surrounding community members move from acquaintances to loved ones, opportunities to share about Jesus will abound (if we are willing to step into these conversations). At the same time, our love for our neighbors is not based on their willingness to respond positively to the Good News. This is why relationship is so vital.

If we view relationships with those in our parish as only a means to an end (i.e., sharing the gospel), then we have slipped into a project-minded approach. People become a task. But the second greatest command does not say, "Love your neighbor as yourself *as long as they don't change the subject when you mention your faith or say no to you when you invite them into a Bible-reading group*." No, the command is to love our neighbors with no ifs, ands, or buts. We do this by proactively welcoming them to learn about Jesus, but our love is not dependent on them accepting our invitation. Instead, we love unconditionally, and as we do, the gospel goes forth, and Christ is honored.

Faithful presence allows followers of Christ to advance the *Kingdom* of Jesus as well. Colossians 1:20 (MSG) says that in Jesus, "all the broken and dislocated pieces of the universe—people and things, animals and atoms—get properly fixed and fit together in vibrant harmonies, all because of his death, his blood that poured down from the cross." One day, Jesus' Kingdom will be fully established, and his worshipers will live with the complete fulfillment of Colossians 1:20. Jesus will reign on the new earth (2 Peter 3:13; Revelation 21:1). And on this new earth, he will reign in a specific place: the Holy City, Jerusalem (Revelation 21:10; 22:1-2). City life will not cease to exist; rather, it will exist in complete perfection apart from sin.

If on the new earth we will not simply return to the Garden but engage in life transcending our current civilizations, then it is incomplete to act as if all that matters in this life is the spiritual. As Matthew 6:10 expresses, Christ longs for his Kingdom to be experienced even now. God is seeking to redeem all aspects of life, including the very systems that form society (education, economics, civic life, and the environment). Jesus wants his Kingdom to be displayed not only at the soul level but also at the systematic level—in every nook and cranny of life—to provide this world with a taste of the full redemption to come. As we learn how to become engaged with and faithfully present in even one of these aspects of life, the Kingdom goes forth and Christ is honored.

Faithful presence allows for disciples of Jesus to advance both the gospel of Christ and his Kingdom. Jesus-followers partnering in the neighborhood must care for and seek to lovingly engage with the spiritual needs of the people who live around them. If they only attend to righting the injustices of their parish or making their place better without sharing the gospel, then the witness of Jesus is incomplete. At the same time, we must remember that our eternal life in the Kingdom will involve not only our souls.

How we engage now with all aspects of life provides the broken world around us with a picture of the reality to come and an invitation to be a part of it. In his book *Until Justice and Peace Embrace*, Nicholas Wolterstorff speaks of the new Jerusalem that is yet to be. He says that in the future picture of Jerusalem, "we have the assurance that our efforts to make these present cities of ours humane places in which to live—efforts which so often are frustrated, efforts which so often yield despair—will, by way of the mysterious patterns of history, eventually provide the tiles and timbers for a city of delight."[2]

For the sake of the here and now, for the sake of the one-day-to-come, and for the sake of the honor of Christ, we urge Jesus-followers partnering in the neighborhood to practice faithful presence in the places where they live. Only then will the broken world around us have a tangible, more complete expression of Christ's Good News and his Kingdom.

Bible Study

God had a plan for the Israelites. While they were in bondage in Egypt, God did not simply see slaves; he saw a future nation. But a nation needs three major components in order to exist: people, law, and land. Through many twists and turns, the nation of Israel was eventually birthed. God had a people (the Israelites), a law (the Ten Commandments and then some), and land (Canaan, eventually called Israel). And once established in Canaan, God did not simply see a nation; he saw a witness to his name.

Before your group meets, pull out some colored pencils and then read the following passage by Moses as he prepares the Israelites to enter the Promised Land for the first time:

> See, I have taught you decrees and laws as the LORD my God commanded me, so that you may follow them in the land you are entering to take possession of it. Observe them carefully, for this will show your wisdom and understanding to the nations, who will hear about all these decrees and say, "Surely

this great nation is a wise and understanding people." What other nation is so great as to have their gods near them the way the LORD our God is near us whenever we pray to him? And what other nation is so great as to have such righteous decrees and laws as this body of laws I am setting before you today?

DEUTERONOMY 4:5-8

1. Underline the words *decrees/laws* in green, *land* in purple, and *people/nation* in orange. Place a red box around the phrase "to the nations." Where are the Israelites supposed to follow the decrees and laws taught by Moses (verse 5)?

_____

_____

2. What is the purpose given for carefully observing the decrees and laws (verse 6)?

_____

_____

_____

3. How do these observations tie into our conversation about the power of corporate faithful presence within a specific location?

_____

_____

_____

God clearly desired the nations to take notice of his people. The way they lived and interacted with one another—their entire way of life, including the systems of their society—was meant to be a witness to the Lord. After all, as we learn in Genesis 28, God's intent was that all the families of the earth would be blessed through Israel. But exactly how did Israel's faithful presence in the Promised Land provide a witness to the nations? To answer this question, we'll examine the physical borders of the land God gave to his people.

Look at the map below.

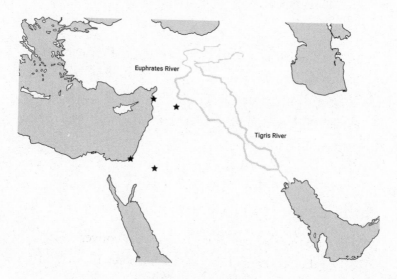

- Four black stars are on the map. Use a red pencil to connect the stars and form a rectangle. Then write the word ISRAEL inside. This rectangle roughly represents the boundaries of Israel in the Ancient Near East.

- Lightly shade the area to the right of our rectangle and beneath the Euphrates River in brown. Then write the word DESERT on top.

- Lightly shade the area directly left of our rectangle in blue. Then write the word WATER on top.

4. After looking at the map, what observations do you make about the physical placement of God's people?

_____

_____

At first it may seem as if God isolated the Israelites from the rest of the known world. After all, with a sea to its west and a desert to its east, Israel didn't seemingly have many close neighbors. In reality, however, isolation was the furthest thing from God's mind.

Water navigation was not well developed during this time, so bypassing Israel by way of the Mediterranean Sea was not an option. With a desert to the east, one could not bypass Israel in that way either. In this respect, Israel was a land bridge that connected all of the major nations in the Ancient Near East. All nations wanting to trade and do business with one another would have to pass through Israel, and during their travels, they got a front-row seat to the laws and customs that God established for his people.[3]

By living a lifestyle of obedience to Yahweh in the

Promised Land, the Israelites, through their everyday lives, provided a glimpse of God to the nations. There are many scriptural examples where God sent people out to proclaim his message, but for the average Israelite, it was ordinary life in their "neighborhood" that gave them a platform to display the goodness of God to the world.

Time Together

Group Discussion Questions
led by facilitator

1. Define *faithfulness* in your own words. Would people tend to describe you as a faithful person? Why or why not?

2. When you picture what it might look like for you to practice faithful presence in your parish, what images or ideas come to mind?

3. How important do you think it is that believers who live in a particular parish engage in one of the following aspects of the community: education, economics, civic life, or the environment? Why do you think this?

4. Which do you tend to be most passionate about and why: the gospel of Jesus or the Kingdom of Jesus? Explain.

Group Activity
led by facilitator

Father Boyle (also known as G-Dog) is a Jesuit priest who lives and ministers in inner-city Los Angeles among gang members. In 2012, he gave a TEDx Talk called "Compassion and Kinship." Though given years ago, this talk continues to encapsulate the way Father Boyle lives life today. After watching the video, share your initial impressions of the TEDx Talk and discuss the questions that follow.

(Warning: The video contains some rough language. To access the video: Go to YouTube [www.youtube.com] and type "Father Greg Boyle TED Talk" in the search engine. Click on the video that is titled "Compassion and Kinship," dated 2012.)

1. How has faithful presence impacted Father Boyle's life and ministry in Los Angeles?

2. Father Boyle has not chosen to embrace faithful presence in an area of his parish where people look, talk, and live just like him. Instead, he chooses to offer a community of compassion and kinship with the marginalized of his place for the betterment of their welfare and the parish as a whole.

• Who are the marginalized in your community?
• How important do you believe it is to be faithfully present among the marginalized of your own parish?

A Story: Schools, Signs, and Submission

Faithful presence is like a mist. Although it can be seen and felt, it is nearly impossible to hold and contain. In many ways, we can only acknowledge the moment, knowing it disappears as quickly as it arrives. I make no claims in sharing my experience that I have consistently practiced faithful presence in my neighborhood. But I have shared in moments that could only happen by rooting my being in a place. I can only describe them as powerful as they are brief. Faithful presence is about being in a place waiting for the holy to arrive.

Our journey to be known characters in our local school is too long to describe in this space. The tale is filled with the historical sadness of a community and the power of division residing in us all. The simplest description is no one in my neighborhood went to the school. If you asked each family, they would give you a variety of reasons, all tinged with racial bias both blatant and understated. Most of the stories were generalizations because no one had any personal experience of attending.

As we began investigating the school, we found many exciting things happening there. We decided to send our firstborn for kindergarten and then apply for the citywide magnet school the next year. After all, most of our neighbors attended the magnet. However, he was not accepted, and our world turned upside down. In the smallest act of obedience, we stayed another year and decided to apply again at the end of first grade. Most of the year we were involved reluctantly, like would-be escapists. I was like the Houdini of my place, one minute there, the next a puff of smoke.

But a day arrived when I knew I could no longer be the magician's act. After finding myself crying in my closet two years in a row because my child did not get into the magnet school, we made the decision to stop applying. What would it look like if we used all this energy to invest in the school my son now loved?

As I asked the question, the dream of what could be was overshadowed by feelings of fear and loneliness. And fear is an enemy of creativity. It took driving down a two-lane road in the backwoods of Alabama, my Emmaus Road if you will, before I could understand faithful presence.

Maybe God does not write his instructions in the sky, but I do believe he is partial to church signs on Highway 43. One day I went for a drive. For thirty minutes, I confessed all my fears—fears I am still ashamed to admit because of the deep bias they expose. More than anything, I wanted courage. Then I spotted a sign beside a roadside church. It read simply, "Courage is fear that has said its prayers."

And there, in that curve of the road, was God's faithful presence acknowledging me as I acknowledged him. His regard for me in that swift moment was enough to begin a journey, a step into a promised land where he had already prepared a place for us. My son is finishing his last year at the neighborhood school, and some days the Kingdom comes rolling in like a mist. It is so delightful when I suddenly see him there among those beautiful faces and faithful teachers. Some would say we are participators in our place, but I would like to hope we are anticipators in place—people who wait with a heart not troubled and eyes that see and know the Father in the mist.

—Lesley, Tuscaloosa, Alabama

- What barriers might you have to overcome in order to love the neighbors in your parish who might take you out of your comfort zone?

3. In what ways does Father Boyle's ministry advance both the gospel of Jesus and the Kingdom of Jesus?

4. What might faithful presence look like for you personally as you engage with your immediate neighbors?

5. What might faithful presence look like for you as a group in your wider parish?

6. What is one practical application that you are willing to commit to as a result of this video and discussion?

Living Up, In, and Out

Your life and my life flow into each other as wave flows
into wave, and unless there is peace and joy and freedom
for you, there can be no real peace or joy or freedom for
me. To see reality—not as we expect it to be but as it
is—is to see that unless we live for each other and in and
through each other, we do not really live very satisfactorily;
that there can really be life only where there really is,
in just this sense, love.

FREDERICK BUECHNER, *The Magnificent Defeat*

So far on our journey together, we've looked at how place matters to God; we've seen how God uses the particularity of our own contexts to form us even as we partner with others to transform our place. Last week we considered how faithfully listening to the Spirit of God is important. We show up, but God does the work. This final week of part 1 will give us a framework for understanding the necessary rhythms of life together in community.

On Your Own

As discussed in week one, once a group of believers decides to live as a community in a specific place, the "very good-ness" of God can be felt and experienced not only by those communing together but also by those who witness and experience that community from a distance. Of course, nobody is promising that committing to life in the **parish** with other believers means nothing but sunshine and roses from that point forward. Far from it! But a group of disciples sharing everyday life together under the grace of God gives the saved and unsaved alike a taste of the Father's Kingdom on earth as it is in heaven.

Still, the questions eventually become, "Yes, we want to commit to one another in a specific place, but what exactly does this mean? How do we pattern our lives after Christ's *together*?"

When I (Julie) was fourteen years old, I decided to apply for the youth missions program at my church. The program was quite a commitment: If each student completed the program, the same group of high school students would end up spending six weeks on mission together for three summers in a row.

At that age, I had never been on a missions trip, and I had no idea what to expect. After the first summer, however, I already knew that I would be signing up for the following two years. Those six weeks after my high school freshman year profoundly influenced my understanding of what it means to be a disciple of Christ and forever affected the way that I would live my life for the Lord.

As I reflect on that experience, I can pinpoint three elements of those trips that helped to make them so meaningful. First, we spent time with Jesus. Every day, our team read our Bibles. We did this separately in the mornings, and each day we spent time as a group reading and praying with one another. We memorized Scripture together, and we naturally talked about the Bible throughout the day. As a result, our passion to know Jesus deepened.

Second, we spent time with one another. To spend six weeks away from home with a group of other young Christ-followers was a unique gift. These friends challenged and encouraged me, and we also had lots of fun. Those first six weeks bonded us together, and that time set a foundation that allowed our relationships to grow deeper as we entered back into "normal life" and began to journey through the rest of high school together.

Finally, we spent time focused on Kingdom purposes. Almost every day our group was out engaging in spiritual conversations with those who did not know the Lord. Each day we spent hours serving people as well as listening to their confusion, arguments, and misunderstandings about God and his Word. These conversations revealed to us the things we ourselves still didn't know about the faith we proclaimed, which in turn drove us back to Scripture. Because of this, we began to learn how to share the love and truth of the gospel with both our actions and words.

I believe that one of the reasons this experience affected me so much was that we invested heavily in relationships similar to those Jesus himself valued when he walked the earth. Let's take a look at Scripture to see what I mean.

Bible Study

Read Luke 6:12-19.

1. Who was Jesus interacting with in verse 12?
   (Reflect on John 10:30 to better understand this
   relationship.)

   _____

   _____

2. As a result of his time praying, what was Jesus' next
   action (verse 13)?

   _____

   _____

3. Read John 15:15. Jesus spoke these words to his
   twelve disciples after they had journeyed together for
   some time. How did Jesus view his relationship to his
   disciples?

   _____

   _____

4. In Luke 6:17, Jesus was with the Twelve, a large crowd of
   his disciples, and who else?

   _____

   _____

5. How did Jesus interact with this third group of people (verses 18-19)?

_____

_____

_____

This passage in Luke shows whom Jesus focused on: the heavenly Father, his disciples, and those who were not yet his followers. In their book, *Building a Discipling Culture*, Mike Breen and Steve Cockram refer to these relationships as *Up*, *In*, and *Out*. *Up* alludes to Jesus' relationship with the Father, *In* to his chosen disciples, and *Out* to the broken world around him. As the authors point out, "This three-dimensional pattern for living a balanced life is evident throughout Scripture. . . . We see these three dimensions in Jesus' lifestyle throughout the Gospels."[1] Choose one of the following passages to read. Note where you see elements of *Up*, *In*, and *Out*.

• Matthew 17:1-18

_____

_____

_____

_____

• Luke 22:39-51

_____

_____

_____

_____

To pattern our lives after the Lord, we should seek to balance these relationships in our lives. But this shouldn't simply be an individual endeavor. The very nature of *In* implies that Jesus made a point of living in community, but it's important to note that this community spilled into his *Up* and *Out* relationships as well. Jesus pulled away to spend time alone, and he even experienced loneliness; however, his life was not lived in isolation.

Think about it: Jesus is the Son of God and was capable of being completely self-sufficient while on earth. He touched people, and diseases were healed; he spoke, and storms obeyed him. Jesus knew his Father so intimately that he said and did exactly what the Father wanted. He had no need to invite others into his relationship with the Father, yet he did so by purposefully allowing his disciples to observe, question, and participate with him as he interacted with his Abba. Likewise, Jesus had no need for help in his public ministry, yet he chose to minister within a community. He lived a three-dimensional life *together with others*, and if we are going to pattern our lives after his, then we need to be willing to do the same with our believing brothers and sisters. When a community of disciples commits to this way of life together in a parish, it is indeed very good.

—*Amber, Columbia, Maryland*

Time Together

Group Discussion Questions

led by facilitator

1. As you think about your own life, which of these three spheres of relationship—*Up*, *In*, or *Out*—is the strongest right now, and which one currently needs the most strengthening? Why do you say this?

2. When you consider incorporating an *Up*, *In*, and *Out* lifestyle alongside other Christ-followers, what excites you about the thought? Does anything make you hesitant or apprehensive?

3. Consider for a moment the possibility of living a three-dimensional life with other believers *in your parish*. What strengths and skills do you have that could help a group of Christ-followers lean into one (or all) of these spheres of relationship? How might proximity aid in this type of lifestyle?

4. What sacrifices might a group of individuals need to make in order to live *Up*, *In*, and *Out* in a parish with other followers of Jesus?

5. Look at the past two weeks of your calendar. Where did your schedule reflect *Up*, *In*, and *Out*, and did any of this time involve engagement in your local community? If necessary, what adjustments might you be able to make in the weeks ahead to better pattern your lifestyle after Jesus' three-dimensional way of living?

Group Activity
led by facilitator

Imagine that each of you has a personal journal and that you are about to write an entry. Pretend that it is three years in the future, and date the entry as such.

For this exercise, picture what your life in your parish might look like if you were living a balanced *Up*, *In*, and *Out* lifestyle alongside other Christ-followers. Assume that you are experiencing wholeness and fulfillment in each of these three areas, and write your entry based on this assumption. Below are some questions to help jump-start your journal entry, if needed:

• What is happening in your heart?

A Story: Up, In, and Out in Committed Community

From 2015 to 2017, I lived in a neighborhood with a community of believers known as Duckanberry. This community began in the most simple way: eating together. In 2010, five guys decided to be intentional about eating dinner together once a week. Shortly thereafter, a neighboring girls' house joined in, and thus the regular rhythm of Monday Night Dinner began, and a community was born.

While some may view dinner together and a community of friends as just a regular social hangout session, a deeper purpose and mission lay within our community. Just as Christ shared life and identity with his disciples, so we shared an identity both individually and corporately given to us through Christ. Living into that shared identity allowed us to collectively be the tangible expression of Christ to those immediately around us: our neighbors. What, then, did this look like? We began regular rhythms in our place that allowed for regular connection while also making space for freedom to be creative and reach out.

During Jesus' time on earth, he regularly met with his Father. At Duckanberry, this rhythm took on different expressions at different times. From studying the book of Ephesians together to praying together on weekday mornings to Sunday night worship times to girls' weekly Bible studies, we at Duckanberry implemented regular patterns of focusing on God together.

In addition to spending time with his Father, Christ also invested much time in his disciples. What did this rhythm look like at Duckanberry? In addition to Monday Night Dinners, we would often randomly gather at one house for breakfast on Saturday mornings. Through these meals, movie nights, and parties, we enjoyed each other's company and felt free to simply relax together.

Within this facet of life, there was much excitement: babies born, engagements announced, birthdays celebrated, weddings planned, and snow days enjoyed to the max. We also shared the difficult times in life.

When one person would move, the rest walked through the transition with him. When relationships ended, the body of Christ at Duckanberry had the opportunity to comfort. When death affected one, it affected us all.

When we shared life together, we were more aware of each other's needs and could work together to meet those needs, whether they were emotional, physical, or spiritual. When one person felt stressed over work and other activities, we had the opportunity to encourage through simple things like laughing together or writing notes of encouragement. While living in Duckanberry, I was regularly challenged and encouraged to grow in my faith through being discipled and discipling others.

Beyond a focus on God and on the body of believers, we sought to consistently reach out and share life with those around us. In his time on earth, Jesus led his disciples in reaching out to others. This pattern for Duckanberry took on the form of quarterly service times at the local food bank. We worked together and also invited not-yet-believing neighbors to join in the service. Through a car wash for the neighbors and a work day at a local family's home, we came together to meet the needs of those around us. In addition to serving neighbors and local families, we invested time in training to fight human trafficking in our parish. We also spent a day simply cleaning and organizing a home and having a cookout with those working in our area to fight social injustice.

Beyond these organized times, I can think of multiple occasions when we just lived out a Christlike life together in front of our neighbors. From starting a food chain for a neighbor family who was suffering physically to blessing a neighbor with a mixer simply because she mentioned she would like to have one to praying over those who were ill, loving our neighbors became more a way of life and less a scheduled event.

While I no longer live in Duckanberry, I often reflect on my time there as inspiration and encouragement to live out these rhythms in my new neighborhood with my husband. Seeking to connect with believers around us gives us stamina and excitement to live like Christ with them while being the tangible expression of Christ to our neighbors.

- What is happening in your neighborhood now that wasn't three years ago?
- How has your view of loving your neighbor as yourself expanded?
- In what ways is your personal life different now than it was three years ago?
- How do you spend your free time differently?
- How has bringing intentionality to each of these spheres of relationship changed your connection with your parish and the people in it?

Allow about fifteen minutes for everyone to write their journal entry, and then have each person share what they wrote. Permit the group to ask questions about each entry and/or reflect on what they enjoyed. Finally, spend some unhurried time in prayer for one another, asking the Lord to bring into fulfillment some of the hopes and dreams that were shared.

PART 2

The Practices of Committed Community Life

Moving Up

Worship Practices That Work in the Neighborhood

> *You and I have been invited to swim with this*
> *Eternal Current for the sake of the world. Jesus*
> *didn't merely invite us to believe about the River. . . .*
> *The invitation is to wade into the River and swim.*
> AARON NIEQUIST, *The Eternal Current*

The last five weeks of our journey together have grounded us in the scriptural basis for partnering together on behalf of our **parish**. As we have moved along, we have also introduced some new terms. Through it all, we hope that you have discovered how **Committed Communities** are a beautiful way that God can draw people toward himself and pour out his goodness in our parishes. However, these concepts aren't meant to be theoretical! These ideas are rooted in tangible practices that happen in our everyday lives. This week we pivot, and the conversations in the remainder of *Finding Home* will get very practical. In week six, we examine how *Up* practices can look on a neighborhood level.

On Your Own

One of my (Stephanie) husband's goals was to complete a triathlon before he turned forty. Ed ran track in college, so training to run wasn't a problem. A road bike purchased off Craigslist got him started bicycling. The swim would, however, be more of a challenge; my husband could stay afloat, but he had never learned how to move effectively or efficiently through the water. He couldn't swim competitively.

First, Ed ordered a book on the particulars of triathlon swimming. Then he watched YouTube videos of people efficiently swimming for a triathlon. But of course, this was insufficient. Ultimately, he had to get into the water and train. He had to practice. He had to be bad at swimming in order to become good. So he scheduled swim days and faithfully showed up at the pool. And he learned to swim. On race day, he finished the course.

Sometimes believers approach gathering as a church as a time to acquire information—the sermon becomes the central purpose of the gathering. But imagine how the triathlon would have gone for my husband had he stopped preparing for the swim after reading a book. Knowledge was important but totally insufficient. Practice is necessary. We encourage you to learn, as my husband did. But before you learn too much, we encourage you to practice. Faith must take shape in the real world in just the same way that swimming is enacted in water. Theory is insufficient; it is time to swim.

Most of the remainder of this tool will be used to present

options for practices that will function like swim lessons for disciples looking to commit together to be in community for the sake of the world, starting in their neighborhood. Some of these practices will be familiar, others will stretch us outside our own traditions. Many of these practices are very old, and some are nearly forgotten. It is unlikely that communities will adopt all of these practices. But it is our sincere hope that as followers of Jesus partner together for their neighborhoods and cultivate unique identities, they will adopt practices that move *Up* in worship, *In* toward shepherding the community they are in, and *Out* into the world that Jesus loves. Experiment. Be willing to stretch and even feel a little silly. Join Jesus in the Eternal Current—participate in his Kingdom come. Jump in; the water is great, and the adventure is unparalleled.

Christ-focused Committed Community is distinct from other forms of intentional community; commitment to Christ is central and binds the community together. Worship, then, is a primary formational and unifying practice. For many, these worship practices will be new. Most people have a way of worship that comes from their own spiritual tradition. For many, that means an evangelical Protestant congregational worship experience. But "four rock songs and a hymn" on Sunday morning is a very narrow and relatively recent worship practice that doesn't always translate to the neighborhood.[1] Even having a "quiet time" is a relatively new worship practice in terms of church history. So how has the global church of God worshiped together through the centuries? What can be learned from believers in other times and places? And how do we bring this worship to gatherings in our neighborhood?

Potential Worship Practices in the Neighborhood

ENGAGING SCRIPTURE IN THE NEIGHBORHOOD

The Reformation theology of the priesthood of all believers was a turning point in church history. It challenged old notions that only the religious elite could approach God and interpret his Holy Scripture. But often when followers of Jesus gather, one person is elected teacher and acts as the expert who lays scriptural truths out for the rest. For ordinary neighbors without faith backgrounds, this can leave little safe space to participate, and it is not always helpful for friends with doubts. So how can worship through Scripture be engaged in the neighborhood?

Here is a strategy, learned from my friend Mark Case, that has borne fruit time and time again. Our community gathers; two people are elected as readers. We use the YouVersion Bible App. A passage is read in one translation of the Bible. Then the second person reads the same text using another translation. Then someone sets a timer for five minutes. The "rule" is that the first five minutes of discussion are given to questions: "I wonder . . . ," "Isn't it strange that . . . ," "What do you think he meant when . . . ," "Do you think he was angry?," "What does that word even mean?" We commit to five full minutes of only questions.

This practice promotes curiosity and humility. It levels the playing field. No one gets to be the expert; no one gets to spout prescriptive solutions. We all wonder together. And we trust that the Holy Spirit will be our teacher and that, in fact, all believers are priests.

After the five minutes of questions pass, the conversation is opened up to pursue a particular question or insight. I always wonder if things will stall out here, or if our conversation will be rudderless without a human guide. Every single time, the Spirit of God seems to direct the conversation. Scripture read orally to a community and engaged in by the community has ancient roots. When we engage Scripture as a community, we join in a long historical tradition. And more importantly for our purposes, this model can easily be implemented in the neighborhood.

BREAKING BREAD—WORSHIP AROUND A TABLE

Shared meals and breaking bread are central practices in nearly every Christian tradition from the first century on. My community has begun to explore the expansiveness of a shared meal around a table as a sacramental practice. We remember that a sacrament is purely an outward expression of an inward grace, and keeping that in mind, we experiment with ways that sharing food together can be worship.

A shared meal as neighbors and followers of Jesus is a way to remember God's extravagant love in a posture of gratitude. And this, we propose, can happen in a number of ways.

Sometimes breaking bread looks like this:

- Shared weekly meals, at which we take a moment to recount God's **faithful presence** in the past week. We wonder and expect God's activity in the coming week. Worship looks like simple conversation, and yet . . . something divine happens around the table.

- We take bread and wine into our physical bodies to remind us of God's presence all around us and Jesus' transformative presence within us. We do this in a way similar to Communion in a traditional evangelical church service. Breaking bread together in traditional Communion reminds us that we are part of a universal church that spans the globe.

- We invite friends outside our own faith tradition to share a meal with us. This is an expression of faith and hospitality. Jesus offers a broad invitation to meet him at the table, so we do as well.

- We bake Christmas cookies and deliver them to our elderly neighbors, thanking them for their presence in our neighborhood.

- We pick fruit from a tree and make lemon curd and jams to share. We wonder at God's provision.

- At other times, our worship through breaking bread masquerades as a neighborhood barbecue or a household of teenagers eating chips and hamburgers.

Some might argue that these things are not sacred at all. But couldn't all these things be done with an attitude of worship? I offer our community's wide practices as an invitation for others to experiment with worship practices of their own. This is the formula we use:

> *People of God + Practicing Gratitude for the Atoning Work of God + Shared Food = Practical Worship in the Neighborhood*

SILENCE AND SOLITUDE

God still speaks. His promises are personal, and his counsel is intimate. He also speaks universally, and politically, and globally. But the buzz and rumble of the twenty-first century drowns out his often-gentle whisper. If we want to hear God, we need to be still and get quiet. This can be done individually, but there is something particularly sacred about a Committed Community setting their intentions together to be still enough to hear the voice of God.

The practices of silence and solitude are so counter to American culture that most of us struggle with this individually, let alone collectively. For the brave, I offer this experiment in worship: Commit and set aside a two- to three-hour window as a Committed Community. Arrange the necessary childcare off site. Then commit to gathering for silence in someone's home. Lay these ground rules: Consider dimming the lights. Set expectations that each person should enter the home without knocking. The community should not greet each other upon arrival; rather, each person should find a comfortable spot and be still before the Lord for an entire hour. The idea is not to bring an agenda to God in prayer but rather to sit quietly in his presence with no agenda at all. After an hour of silence, the host should break the quiet with a prayer and ask, "What have you heard from the Lord?" Spend the next hour processing the time of silence aloud as a community. If time allows, share dinner or dessert.

EXAMEN

This four-hundred-year-old Ignatian prayer practice can be done alone or with others in community. It is a way to notice the work and presence of God.

Here is the outline of a basic Examen prayer practice: First, allow a moment to become aware of the Spirit of God present with you. Then each person should take several minutes to review his or her day in gratitude, quietly to himself or herself. After intentionally looking at the day through a lens of gratitude, everyone should pay attention to the strongest one or two emotions of the day, either positive or negative. Ask God what he is saying through that feeling. Then choose one feature of the day (large or very small) and pray about that portion of the day, listening to what God has to say about it. Finally, spend a moment considering the next day, asking God that you might be sensitive to his presence in the coming day.

This prayer practice works best in a group when there is a facilitator. If no one in your community feels comfortable with this, I highly recommend a liturgy of Examen developed by A New Liturgy[2] and facilitated by Father Michael Sparough. It's available at the following link: https://store.anewliturgy.com /album/no-6-the-examen-extended-edition. You may listen several times for free; after that, this fantastic liturgical tool is available for a small fee.

A Prayer Walk Story:
Worship Practices in the Neighborhood

Before I moved to Seattle from a suburban neighborhood in Michigan, I never thought that I would be living in a place with such diversity. Concrete sidewalks, nature trails, bus routes, small neighborhood businesses, family homes, a smorgasbord of people, and even a community garden all now remind me that this is indeed the place that God has chosen for my wife and me in this season of our lives. Rain or shine, residing here has become a gift that we treasure.

But moving across the country was a big change, and falling in love with my neighborhood was a process. The love I feel for my neighborhood has been cultivated over time and facilitated by a spiritual practice I call my "prayer walk."

During my two-mile prayer walk, I've lost track of how many people I have met. Sometimes we share a quick hello or a simple nod, but often the encounters evolve into the sharing of personal stories. As I walk and pray, I focus on four words: soften, center, listen, and respond. These words remind me to soften my heart and center on Jesus. They remind me to listen to the Spirit and to my neighborhood and then be willing to respond to what I hear.

As I walk, I have places where I pause and specifically pray for different things. My first stop is what I call the Psalm 1 tree—a beautiful western red cedar that sits next to Longfellow Creek. Here I place my hand on the tree and pray for my wife, for each of our children, for their spouses, and for our grandchildren.

Then I continue my walk along a winding hiking trail, "listening" for his whispers and his guidance and "responding" to his presence and his Word. I am learning that God cares deeply about four areas of every city: education, environment, local economy, and civic leaders. So as I continue my walk along the trail, I pray for these four areas. I pray that

God's Kingdom will grow and that his will be done, here in my neighborhood, on earth as it is in heaven.

When I leave the trail, I enter a more urban cityscape. I come to a bus stop, so I pray for the teachers and the students in the school in front of me. My next stop is at a local business, a small market. The owner has become a dear friend. My final destination is our local community garden. There is a sign that reads "Welcome to Your Neighborhood"; often, a neighbor is working in one of the plots. What a beautiful word picture! Much like the plants that are growing, friendships and the gospel are spreading.

As I finish my walk back home, I pray and meet neighbors along the way.

The words soften, center, listen, and respond continue to guide me the rest of my day as I pray that I will live with radical love and full inclusion. These four words, coupled with countless steps throughout my neighborhood, continue to be one of the most life-giving spiritual practices of my faith journey: the prayer walk.

I invite you to share with me in my neighborhood liturgy and begin a prayer walk in your own parish. "Today, if you hear his voice, do not harden your hearts" (Hebrews 4:7).

—Kirk, Seattle, Washington

Time Together

Group Discussion Questions
led by facilitator

1. What is your personal history with worship practices? Did you grow up in a faith tradition or without one? How has this influenced you?

2. Everyone finds some worship practices to be more meaningful than others. Some find being alone in nature inspires worship. Others love to worship with music. Still others find it most powerful to worship in large congregations. Some love the tradition of high church; others prefer new worship expressions. What is your preference? What types of worship stretch you the most?

3. What type of worship that you have never practiced are you most curious about? How would you like to experiment in worship? Or conversely, how would you like to commit to practice a type of worship already in your repertoire more regularly?

Group Activity
led by facilitator

- Use a phone to play "An Abbreviated Examen Liturgy" (available at https://store.anewliturgy.com/track

/an-abbreviated-examen-liturgy). Let this track guide your group through a shared prayer of Examen. Discuss the experience afterward.

- For further study, research the practice of *lectio divina* and spend some time engaging Scripture in this manner during the next week. This may be done as a group or individually.

Moving In

Learning Rhythms of Authentic Relationship

To love at all is to be vulnerable. Love anything, and your heart will certainly be wrung and possibly be broken. If you want to make sure of keeping it intact, you must give your heart to no one, not even to an animal. Wrap it carefully round with hobbies and little luxuries; avoid all entanglements; lock it up safe in the casket or coffin of your selfishness. But in that casket—safe, dark, motionless, airless—it will change. It will not be broken; it will become unbreakable, impenetrable, irredeemable.

C. S. LEWIS, *The Four Loves*

Last week we looked at worship practices that translate to a neighborhood context and offered them as a buffet of options for **Committed Communities** in the **parish**. We dubbed these *Up* practices, as they keep communities looking up in worship. But if this is all a Committed Community does, it will be malformed. This week's practice looks at how we can be in faithful relationship with others in our community. We call it "Moving In."

On Your Own

The other year, my (Julie) daughter started preschool. It's not every day that she tells me about her interactions with the other kids in her class, but sometimes she gives me insight into her schoolmates' personalities. As she walks me through her days, I have come to learn that there is a boy who loves to make jokes, a girl who tends to cry a lot, and another child who is very shy but sweet. Though each child has unique qualities, these individual kids have learned how to function together as a class. In the beginning of the school year, they were unknown to one another; now they are known by each other, and they operate together to learn and have fun.

Remember *your* childhood schoolmates? It's possible that some faces are popping into your mind right now. Most of us probably recall the boy who was so smart that he ruined the grading curve for everyone else, or the girl who got picked first in gym class because of her athleticism, or the awkward kid who was socially banned by the majority. Yet somehow, regardless of cliques and a wide range of personalities, each year, you and your classmates forged through school together, experiencing the highs and lows of certain teachers, projects, exams, and school events.

Children don't get to choose who their classmates are. When they reach a certain age, most kids attend a public school, and from that moment on, they must figure out how to relate to the other students and get along. This is easier for some than others, but on a grand scale, most children find their way and begin to form some relationships that blossom into friendships.

And then we grow up.

Something changes for most people after high school and

college. We may move to an area that we think will best suit our needs, yet we often find ourselves leaving our local contexts to spend time elsewhere. Our recreational activities, our friends, even our churches often pull us away from our parish and the people in it.

To live in Committed Community within a parish, we must be willing to be present and lean into relationship with those who are like-hearted in their love of God and others. Like children who enter school for the first time, you likely do not get to choose who lives around you. But as an adult living in a specific parish, you can choose to whom you offer your loyalty and love. And once you choose to walk in a committed relationship with other Christ-followers, it is up to you—collectively—to move from unknown to known, from individuals to an extended family that operates together to worship, spur one another on, and usher in the Kingdom of God.

And so, let the swimming lessons continue.

The Rhythms of In

Richness in relationship does not happen overnight. There are no shortcuts; it takes time and intentionality for relationships to grow and develop. Let's pause here for a moment to reflect on this.

Jesus spent lots of time with his Committed Community. At first, the Twelve knew Jesus in a formal sense, as rabbi. But do you remember John 15:15? Jesus said that he no longer called his disciples servants but friends. Verse 12 reveals to us that Jesus loved these twelve men. And no wonder! Think of all they did together: prayed, healed people, combatted the religious leaders, discussed Scripture, attended Jewish festivals, and went to temple, to name a few. But beyond these more formal affairs, these men spent time simply living life together. They ate in each other's homes, attended weddings, visited friends (remember Lazarus?), went fishing, sat around campfires, and pulled away from the crowds for some guy time.

Through Jesus' example, we see that both the **calculated** (formal or planned) **moments** and **casual** (informal or spontaneous) **moments** matter in building camaraderie. Committed Communities require regular shared times together that are guarded in the calendar; but without the relaxed—and sometimes even unplanned—moments, a community will not thrive.

The goal of viewing these relationships through the lens of the calculated and the casual is not to be formulaic. Communities are not static; they will, and should, change over time. Recognizing the need for balance in our *In* rhythms allows space for Committed Communities to grow and develop. Each group should feel the freedom to experiment and change practices so that they can best care for and enjoy one another.

Look again at the quote at the beginning of week six. When it comes to leaning into community, some of us may feel like we're standing on the riverbank, not sure if we even want to

A Story:
Committed Community Moves into the Neighborhood

A group of Christ-followers in Detroit, Michigan, has learned the value of moving In—literally! The following story will give you a glimpse into the everyday rhythms of this Committed Community.[1]

When Matt and Bev Hale moved to Detroit in 2003 to start a holistic urban ministry, everything rested on humility. "I would call our first few years more unlearning than learning," Matt says. "I didn't realize how much I had taken certain aspects of my own culture to be part of the gospel." The Hales' ministry centers around a community God built from the humble ground up. As the Hales and the other residents live together in formerly foreclosed homes they've restored, sharing the everyday—meals, gardening, studying the Word, worshiping, discussing faith, and sharing struggles—Matt sees family being born. What started with Matt and Bev and one house grew to four houses and twenty-three diverse people living in intentional community at the center of one of the most racially divided cities in America.

Road to Reconciliation. *"For Detroit, our community is a unique thing," Matt says. "There are few places you can go in Detroit that are not all black or all white. There is deep racial division in the metro area, and you feel it." You can feel it at the six-foot concrete wall separating the old black and white neighborhoods. After seven decades, it still stands. "Ephesians 2:14 says, 'For he himself is our peace, who has made the two groups one and has destroyed the barrier, the dividing wall of hostility,'" Matt says. "Jesus is central to reconciliation in any form. He destroys the dividing wall."*

Matt and Bev want their living community to be a picture of Christ-broken barriers.

Meeting Needs, Healing Hearts. *Sometimes the struggles are more than they can handle. That's where God always provides. One of the*

Hales' most valuable partners, Central Detroit Christian Community Development Corporation, has been ministering in Detroit for more than twenty years. Many of the Hales' community's residents work or volunteer for the corporation, providing job training, housing, youth programs, and food and gardening programs to Detroit's urban poor. "We realized our strength was in relationships, and not necessarily in programs," Matt says. "But we also realized those programs were really necessary for our community. It's hard to sit in somebody's house and share the gospel when their lights are cut off and there's no food in the fridge. The gospel is true, and it's the way to the Kingdom, but you can't skip over those felt needs."

More than Housemates, More than a House. *When community resident ShaCha graduated from college, she chose to stay in her native Detroit. By joining the Hales' community, ShaCha not only met her soon-to-be husband, she found an entire extended family. "This community has loved me, rebuked me, served me, healed me, and walked beside me," ShaCha says. "In this individualistic, shallow society, our dedication and love for one another often draws people craving something deeper." Today, ShaCha runs a leadership program in public schools as well as a racial-reconciliation consultation company.*

Another community member, Nate, also sees this intentional community as a change agent in his life. "Healthy Christian community is a reflection of God's grace," Nate says. "The Lord walks with us and loves us in spite of our sin. That same spirit is needed in community to continue to love one another when our faults are evident."

Community member Kori sees the group as a revelation of God's handprints in all of life.

"Life with other people will feel awkward, aimless, or mundane at times," Kori says. "I am starting to see God in all of that. God is working everywhere, in everything and in everyone. He is showing himself as much in the process as in the arriving."

A Very Old New Thing. *Matt is careful to stress that community has deeper roots than any modern-day ministry. "Living in fellowship is nothing new," Matt says. "It's not a hip fad. It's the oldest way people lived in Christianity." But today, perhaps more than any other time in human history, community attracts. "Many are tired of culture's false connectedness and self-focus. People in poor communities seem more aware that they need each other for survival," Matt says, "that they need God for survival. Wealth gives us this illusion that we are not in need."*

—Matt and Bev,
Detroit, Michigan

dip our toes into the water. Stepping into the River means facing our insecurities about ourselves and others, and that is scary stuff! Past experiences have left some of us feeling beat up and bruised. But may we not let fear strip us of the freedom that God wants us to experience. As we open ourselves up to others, they will not always get it right—*we* will not always get it right! Misunderstandings, hurts, and frustrations will come, but so can grace, forgiveness, restoration, and love.

For those of us who are already in the water, let's continue to let the River refresh and revive us. Let's recognize the beauty of where we are but know that the Great River-Maker has even deeper waters for us to explore and enjoy.

As we begin to reflect on our own *In* relationships, can we all agree to be courageous and take one step deeper into the waters of community? The Kingdom of God does not exist without relationship. Relationship to the King is paramount, but so are our relationships with one another. If we are going to swim in God's River, we must learn to love one another, and what better place to do that than within Committed Community?

Time Together

Group Discussion Questions
led by facilitator

1. It may seem like common sense to write that Christ-followers who are living in the same parish and want to be a Committed Community must spend time together

and learn to care for one another. Why, then, does this seem so difficult at times? What barriers tend to keep disciples who live in the same place from building true, authentic relationships?

2. Below is a list of some *In* practices that Committed Communities around the country live out (notice how *Up* and *Out* practices weave throughout this list):

watching a TV series
serving regularly at a
    local food bank
weekly dinners
monthly prayer nights
    for the neighborhood
going to the pool
celebrating birthdays
writing encouraging notes
board-game nights
monthly soup night

firepit hangouts
pancake breakfasts
neighborhood Halloween
    party
gardening
football-watching parties
Christmas tree–decorating
    party
trash pickup days in the
    community
weekly Bible study

The above list is here to help your juices begin to flow. What *In* practices would you add to this list, based on your context?

3. Discuss one or two practices that you might like to try together as a group. Remember to experiment and have fun! There is no "right" way to enjoy life with one another in the neighborhood.

4. Below is a scale to indicate the two needed spheres
   of interaction for authentic relationship to develop:
   calculated and casual. Individually, place an *X* to
   indicate how you personally tend to spend most
   of your relational energy. If you know each other
   well enough, place another mark on the scale to
   represent how you as a group tend to spend your
   time together.

Calculated   *Casual*

Discuss where you placed your *X*s. If skewed on one side
or the other, what can you do to find a balance between the
calculated and the casual?

5. Not all believers who live in the same parish should
   necessarily move toward becoming a Committed
   Community. Discuss together when it might be
   appropriate for a group to refrain from entering
   into this level of relationship.

Group Activity
led by facilitator

1. Watch the following commercials. You can type in the
   URL address or simply do a Google search using the
   listed titles.

- Christmas Together (Waitrose): https://www.youtube .com/watch?v=in8XhKocXlM
- Eat Together (President's Choice): https://www.youtube .com/watch?v=vDuA9OPyp6I
- Bring Neighbors Together (AncestryDNA): https:// vimeo.com/showcase/4834115/video/286096782
- Open Your World 1 (Heineken): https://www.youtube .com/watch?v=dKggA9k8DKw

According to these advertisements, what hurdles must people overcome in order to get to know one another?

2. Based on these commercials, what are some things that can bring people together or make them feel included?

3. Notice how each advertisement has some element of food or drink directly or indirectly displayed. Pick a date on the calendar to share an unhurried meal with one another. Try to meet in someone's home. Whether a potluck or a sit-down meal provided by one person, the main goal is to be together. Before your meal, have each person write five "Would you rather . . . ?" questions on separate index cards. Place them in a bowl and spend the meal answering these questions. Be ready to engage and simply enjoy a fun evening with one another. Here are some examples of "Would you rather . . . ?" questions to get you started:

- Would you rather hang with a few friends or go to a big party?
- Would you rather go into the past and meet your ancestors or go into the future and meet your great-great-grandchildren?
- Would you rather put a stop to war or end world hunger?
- Would you rather have a cook or a maid?
- Would you rather know how you will die or when you will die?
- Would you rather take a guaranteed $100,000 or a 50/50 chance at $1,000,000?

Moving Out

In Faithful Presence

More and more, the desire grows in me simply to walk around, greet people, enter their homes, sit on their doorsteps . . . and be known as someone who wants to live with them. It is a privilege to have the time to practice this simple ministry of presence. Still, it is not as simple as it seems. . . . It is difficult not to have plans, not to organize people around an urgent cause, and not to feel that you are working directly for social progress. But I wonder more and more if the first thing shouldn't be to know people by name, to eat and drink with them, to listen to their stories and tell your own, and to let them know with words, handshakes, and hugs that you do not simply like them, but truly love them.

HENRI NOUWEN, *Gracias!: A Latin American Journal*

We've discussed *Up* practices that bring worship to the neighborhood, and we've talked about moving *In* toward faithful relationship with other Jesus-followers in **Committed Community**. But a Committed Community would still be as unstable (unhealthy) as a two-legged stool with only these two features. This week, let's discuss how Committed Communities can faithfully move *Out* into the world God loves. After all, healthy Committed Communities move **Up, In, and Out.**

On Your Own

In 1860, the Bureau of Indian Affairs began an experiment in social engineering and deculturation. By the 1880s, over 6,800 native children were enrolled in boarding and day schools with the sole mandate of assimilating these children to "American" life and Western ideals. Thousands of Native American children were forcibly removed and sometimes outright kidnapped from their parents. They were forbidden to speak their native languages, stripped of their traditional clothing, and fed a meager Western diet. Rigid systems and harsh discipline ruled the day. Mornings were spent teaching academics and afternoons were preserved for industrial education. This often led to the children being forced to work in the fields and homes of white families; child labor was thinly veiled as education. Abuse was rampant. The United States government paid missionaries to run these schools, fully intending they would convert children to a Protestant faith.

Christians have not always done this "missionary thing" well. Let us start with that. There are countless stories, horrific religious wars, and arrogant colonization that match or exceed this one in their atrocity and violence.

And yet Paul says, "I am not ashamed of the gospel, because it is the power of God that brings salvation to everyone who believes: first to the Jew, then to the Gentile" (Romans 1:16). The word *gospel* means "good news"; we believe that Jesus, Immanuel—God with us—is in fact very good news. Except, as in the case of missionaries in cahoots with the United States Bureau of Indian Affairs, sometimes "good news" is delivered with a bludgeon. And then we are surprised that people don't receive it well.

Recently, my (Stephanie) daughter participated in a children's choir hosted by a local church and run by some very kind people. She was encouraged to invite family to the final concert, so she did. My in-laws, some very nice agnostic people, happened to be in town and went to support their granddaughter. All went well until the close of the concert when an altar call was given; it was laced heavily with rhetoric of sin, shame, and otherness. Then the offering plate was passed, wherein friends and family were guilted into throwing cash in the plate. The gospel of Jesus was delivered as if it were bad news. Though the hosts of the event had the very best intentions, it felt like a manipulative "bait and switch." These types of Christian events are all too common.

How then shall we live? What do followers of Jesus who choose to partner together for the sake of their community do? The gospel is good news, with the power to transform lives and families. It can transform communities, **built spaces**, economies, and education. But so often, we have done this badly. The answer to reckless action and hurried strategy is in how the people of God abide. Jesus says in John 15:5, "I am the vine; you are the branches. If you remain in me and I in you, you will bear much fruit; apart from me you can do nothing." So the very first thing the people of God need to do is stay near to the heart of Jesus. To know him and how he moved in his community is to begin to discern what posture we should take in our own places and with our own neighbors and friends.

Second, we must abide in our neighborhoods and towns. We must be physically present—walk the streets, shop at the local markets, potentially move our work into our community, plant a garden, and touch the soil of the place. Jesus said, "Where your treasure is, there your heart will be also" (Matthew 6:21). If Jesus-followers want to band together on behalf of their place, they must first begin to love their place like Christ does. They must consider where their treasure abides.

The prophet Jeremiah gave the Jewish exiles a message from God about how they should inhabit their place. Even today, those truths can guide communities of faith as they seek to fall in love with the neighborhood to which God has called them.

> Build houses and settle down; plant gardens and eat what they produce. Marry and have sons and daughters; find wives for your sons and give your daughters in marriage, so that they too may have sons and daughters. Increase in number there; do not decrease. Also, seek the peace and prosperity of the city to which I have carried you into exile. Pray to the LORD for it, because if it prospers, you too will prosper.
>
> **JEREMIAH 29:5-7**

So as the people of God stay near to Jesus and become present in their place, they can trust that the Spirit will guide them into practices that help them embody the Good News in ways that do not feel like bad news. The humble posture of the exile, plus the agency of a beloved child of God, plus the invested heart of a neighbor form the identity capable of **faithful presence** that is good news in the neighborhood. Faithful presence can build bridges of trust with neighbors, bridges that can sustain gospel conversations as they emerge.

But practically, what does this mean? You know the place God has you better than we could. We can tell you what others, after listening to their neighborhood, have chosen to do. Some of these things are very small, others are enormous. We offer them as a smorgasbord of brainstorming opportunities. There is no prescription here, only invitation to wonder. Consider these practices:

- Do a daily prayer walk.
- Bring cookies to a neighbor.
- Share fruit from a tree.
- Plant a garden in the front yard.
- Join the Turquoise Table movement (https://theturquoisetable.com).
- Find a new job within your community.
- Join the parent-teacher association.
- Shop local—buy produce at the farmers' market every week.
- Build a Little Free Library (https://littlefreelibrary.org/).
- Get involved in local government or the homeowners' association.

- Build a tiny home in your backyard for someone experiencing homelessness.
- Volunteer.
- Start a business.
- Join a community-supported agriculture co-op.
- Keep bees.
- Start a book club or Bible study.
- Live in Committed Community.
- Invite your neighbor to dinner.
- Pray for teachers.
- Donate to a local charity.
- Buy coffee from a local coffeehouse instead of a chain.
- Shovel snow in the neighborhood.
- Carpool to work.
- Coach for a local sports league.
- Start a supper club.
- Clean litter from the highway.
- Adopt an elementary school.
- Become a foster parent or join Safe Families (https://safe-families.org/).
- Support a foster parent.
- Drive a sick neighbor to a doctor's appointment.
- Vote.
- Join a local gym.
- Visit a nursing home regularly.

People have done all these things as acts of faithful presence in their neighborhoods. They are largely simple habits

A Story: Years of Faithful Presence

In November 2016, I was helping a neighbor rehang some shutters on their house. My ladder was resting on the sill of a second-floor window. Not wanting to waste time climbing down to reposition the ladder, I began to stretch to fasten the last and farthest screw through the shutter and into the brick. At some point, I lost my handhold and began the twenty-foot drop at a much more accelerated pace than I would have preferred. Later, in the hospital, my doctors reported that I had a burst fracture of my L1 vertebra, as well as a broken leg.

My wife, Patty, and I had spent years investing in our neighborhood and were encouraged by the community that was developing. But I think both of us were wondering where we should go from here. We had good relationships with folks in our neighborhood. Both of us were regularly reading the Bible with neighbors. God was working in significant ways in the lives of a few. But we were wondering about next steps. How do we begin to draw folks together in seeking the shalom of our place? As we began to see turnover in the neighborhood, how could we integrate new homeowners into the fabric of our place?

While I was still in the hospital, Patty and I began to talk about the accident and how it might fit into God's plans and purposes. God gave us a powerful idea. This was an opportunity for our neighborhood to serve and support us. Although we received many offers from our church community and elsewhere, we chose to rely heavily on our neighbors.

Serving folks around us had always been an important element of our neighboring. And we had discovered a principle in serving that we called reciprocity. Often people don't feel comfortable with our efforts to serve them. But if we find ways to allow our neighbors to serve us, it seems to remove the awkwardness of our serving initiatives. My recovery would be long and arduous. We needed help in a big way. And we determined that we would rely on our neighbors to meet that need.

Well, our neighbors came through in the biggest way. They brought meals every other day for more than a month. Neighbors that we hardly knew brought meals more than once. Guys came and moved furniture to make a bedroom on the first floor. When I needed to go to doctors' appointments, they came and carried my wheelchair with me in it out of the house and helped me into the car. I was completely helpless, especially during the first couple of weeks. Patty had the role of nurse thrust upon her in addition to an already busy schedule. Our neighbors filled in the gaps for us in so many ways. Although it was humbling to be so dependent on others, we were encouraged to see our neighborhood function as a real community. And it gave us fuel for affirming those around us. Choosing to be dependent on our neighbors gave them an opportunity to demonstrate the faithful presence that we had been trying to model. And that demonstration of faithful presence on their part enhanced relationships that we had been working on for many years. We experienced the benefits of authentic Committed Community in a powerful way. We will forever be motivated to work toward that kind of community wherever God leads us.

—*Andy, Cincinnati, Ohio*

of investing in the flourishing of the **parish**. Few of them are overtly spiritual, yet we maintain all of them can be deeply so. If the people of God follow the ways of Jesus and show up in their places, the Spirit of God will absolutely be at work. The very good news of Jesus and his Kingdom is at play. After all, Jesus was born in Bethlehem, the town whose name, translated, is "a promise of abundant provision."[1] As believers join the work of Jesus in the neighborhood, we become part of his Kingdom plan to wage abundant provision in our hometowns, streets, and communities.

Time Together

Group Discussion Questions
led by facilitator

1. When have you seen the Good News of Jesus and his Kingdom delivered with a bludgeon? Have you ever been on the receiving end? Have you accidentally participated? There are too many examples of Christians doing missions poorly. Why do you think that is? What can disciples of Jesus do to check their methods?

2. An actionable first step to being present in the parish is to look at where your treasure abides. Is your job in your neighborhood or town? Are your bank and grocery store? Where do you get your hair cut, and where do your children attend school? Do you shop at big-box stores

or local mom-and-pop shops? Do you participate in a community-supported agriculture co-op or community garden? Can some of these patterns change to bring your life more fully into the parish? Can small changes like this make a difference?

3. Faithful presence in the parish or neighborhood requires followers of Jesus to realistically name their limitations and also live fully into their agency and power as neighbors and disciples. What circumstances in your life and neighborhood really do limit you? What might be the blessing in that? What are untapped areas of influence in your neighborhood? Is now the time to begin to use those resources?

Group Activity
led by facilitator

Brainstorm several things you could do together to move *Out* into your parish in faithful presence. They should be large and small, easy and difficult. After you've made the list, ask these questions:

- Does this really fit our context?
- Do we have capacity to engage in this?
- Is there someone in our parish already doing this work whom we can support?

After you've brainstormed and then narrowed down your list, consider choosing one thing you could do to move *Out* into the neighborhood in faithful presence. Begin making a plan to implement this idea.

The Power of Linking

Two are better than one . . . ; for if either of them falls,
the one will lift up his companion. But woe to the one
who falls when there is not another to lift him up!

ECCLESIASTES 4:9-10, NASB

For the last three weeks, we have looked at the practices that form healthy rhythms in **Committed Community** life: **Up. In. Out.** They are the catchphrases that act as a reminder of the types of relationships that foster healthy formation. But there is one more element that helps Committed Communities in the **parish** thrive. It has to do with the strength of building connections across a larger space. This week we will talk about the power of **linking**.

On Your Own

It was true in the Garden, and it is still true today: "It is not good for the man to be alone" (Genesis 2:18). As you live life in your parish, it is essential that you are connected in some way, shape, or form to others who also have a heart for your community. *The New Parish* authors call this proactive practice *linking*.[1] Linking is the practice of growing meaningful relationships with people and places both inside and outside your own parish.

List some reasons right now why linking might be an important practice:

_____

_____

_____

_____

To prevent burnout. To remain creative. To remember that you are not alone. These are just a few reasons why it is important to link with others. And this practice is a relevant one for those who may even already exist within a Committed Community!

Let's flesh this out a bit. Take a look at the figure below. (For the sake of this conversation, we'll assume that our starting position is within a fully functioning Committed Community.)

Each circle indicates a unique form of linking that can take place. Of course, people living as a Committed Community are connected to one another, but engaging with others beyond this sphere will enhance the life of the group as well

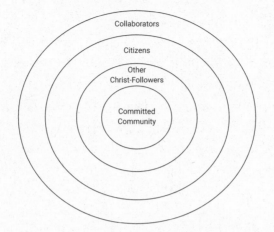

as open up new and exciting possibilities of leaning into the pulse of the neighborhood. And don't let the circles fool you either. Though the rings move further and further out from the center, this does not mean that the relationships on the rim are less important than the ones closest to the center. All are worthwhile and can bring their own vibrancy to you and to the life of your parish.

Christect-Followers[2]

Remember Elijah? This well-known prophet experienced a huge spiritual victory on Mount Carmel in 1 Kings 18. However, it is in this chapter that we learn of a reality that begins to affect Elijah's very soul. In verse 22, Elijah announces to the people of Israel that he is the only one of the Lord's prophets left. In the next chapter, Elijah says the same thing to God two more times. As one reads this account, it becomes more and more clear: Elijah feels alone, and this is depressing him. But it is in this tender moment that God reveals to Elijah that his being alone is only a *perceived* reality. In 1 Kings 19:18, God says, "Yet I reserve seven thousand in Israel—all whose knees have not bowed down to Baal and whose mouths have not kissed him."

Sometimes we can feel alone in our neighborhoods. Focusing on life in the parish is not a common pursuit of the average US citizen, and at times this can give us an "Elijah perception." But God sees all, and he is at work everywhere. Like Elijah in his day, this should give us hope. It should also show us the importance of linking.

In every parish, there are other disciples who long to see the Kingdom of heaven displayed, and they may even be doing some wonderful ministry right in your context. This does not mean that these people must join your Committed Community or that they will look like you and agree with you on every point of theology. Fortunately these things are not essential for linking to happen.

The goals of linking with other Christ-followers in the parish are to (1) encourage one another in each of your pursuits, (2) enjoy the diversity of the body of Christ in your neighborhood, and (3) engage in joint projects or service, if/when appropriate.

Building meaningful relationships with other disciples in your place will help to keep the Elijah perception at bay, and we bet that you will also find yourself encouraged as you get a greater glimpse of all that God is up to in your parish.

Citizens

One day I (Julie) walked with my daughter to a nearby playground. While there, a woman with paper in hand readily told me that she was working to get speed bumps put in along a certain busy road. She believed that people were prone to speed there and that those walking on the sidewalks or trying to cross the street did not feel as safe as they should. This woman needed to find a few community members to sign her petition and be on a committee to make this hope become a reality. Though I was not ready to join a committee, I discovered that one of my nearby neighbors was, so I connected the two women. We still don't have speed bumps, but I now know that there is a group of concerned citizens working to make our streets safer.

There are engaged community members in every parish. These men and women may not be doing their works in the name of Jesus, but sometimes these folks care more about the neighborhood than the average disciple, and it would be wise not to ignore their presence. As with Christ-followers, we can encourage citizens' pursuits that benefit the parish, enjoy the diversity they add to our community, and possibly engage in some like-minded ventures. And sometimes, we may also get to be a part of their spiritual journeys.

We should never view people as projects—the reasons for this are fairly obvious. Yet out of a place of deep caring, we hope that those who live around us might come to know the truth and love of Jesus. Fortunately, God knows each person's heart better than we do, and there are people in every parish who are ready to receive him. How do I know this?

In Luke 10, Jesus describes what has come to be known as **"People of Peace."** These are men and women God has divinely set in place who will be open to his message and willing to use their reputation and connections to help advance efforts that forward his Kingdom. People of Peace are not always easy to find, but they do exist—perhaps even on your street!

Though we do not promote going door to door in order to argue people into a relationship with Jesus, we do support building loving relationships with citizens who also care about your parish. Perhaps God will allow you to sow spiritual seed into the lives of some of these folks. But even if not, at the very least, you will make some new connections in the neighborhood and therefore will better serve your place and the people who live in it.

Collaborators

Did you know that female elephants are good baby-sitters? It's true! Female elephants look after one another's calves; it is a community effort and simply a way of life for a herd.

This babysitting effort has two major results. First, it teaches both the babysitter and the ones being looked after. An article from *The Independent* explains that "Female elephants (cows) help look after each other's calves. Babysitting other female's calves is important for elephant development; young females learn how to look after the young, and the calves are shown how it's done." Second, it protects the very life of a calf. In fact, "The survival rate of a calf greatly increases when more females are present and willing [to] take care of it."[3]

Those committed to life in the parish would be wise to learn from these elephants. Each of us can run the risk of becoming insular. It is possible for individuals and Committed Communities to become so inwardly focused that they turn a blind eye to the greater world around them. But just as there is value in linking with people *within* your place, there is value in linking with others *outside* of your parish. In fact, as with a wild calf, this linking may at times become a matter of survival.

The quote at the beginning of week one said that living with loneliness increases our odds of dying early by 45 percent. In the same way, our "life" in the neighborhood has a chance of being snuffed out early if we go it alone. Doubts can start to creep into our mindset: *Am I crazy for living life this way? Even my local church body doesn't seem to understand. Maybe I've been wrong about all of this.*

Doubt can lead to discouragement, and discouragement can lead to an early "death" in the neighborhood.

This may seem extreme, but you would be surprised at the thoughts and emotions that come when you don't hear anyone cheering you on. Many times people must look beyond their own contexts to hear others say, "Keep going! This way of living life in your parish is an expression of the Kingdom of God. We're with you." This support from others can at times be a lifeline. And like a baby elephant, the more you can link with others who live out the values expressed in this resource, the greater your chances of survival in the long run.

In addition to survival, when a Committed Community is willing to engage with other parishes, ideas for innovation and best practices begin to arise. Meaningful relationships in these spheres help to point out blind spots and provide some much-needed encouragement. This give-and-take between parishes allows Committed Communities not merely to survive but to thrive.

Linking in this way can happen within a city, region, nation, or even globally. Admittedly, at first it may feel a bit overwhelming to take steps in this direction, but don't let this discourage you. Be sure to check appendix B for information on how to contact The Navigators and The Parish Collective. Both desire to help you get connected with others who are present in their communities and seeking to love their neighbors as themselves.

A Story: Threads of Relationship

"The best way for me to love this person is to stay away from them, since we don't really get along!" That is the cheap and easy way to sidestep the radical love that Jesus demonstrated to us and called us to. Tempting as this attitude sometimes is, God is leading me on a winding journey to love my neighbors in very practical ways. This is a rich journey, but it was spiritually isolating, especially in the early years. I found people in my neighborhood who were sharing in valuable work. But that support network didn't come from the church or Christians in the neighborhood; it came from others who did not share my faith. I wasn't relationally isolated; I was spiritually isolated from people who followed Jesus and wanted to tangibly love their neighbors and neighborhood.

In fact, there was a tremendous gap of time where I didn't have peers in my neighborhood who desired to love God and also tangibly love our neighbors. I was motivated by getting to participate in bringing about God's dream for the world, yet this desire was not shared by my church-going neighbors. In my Christian community, I felt like an odd duck. Very few people understood what God was doing in my neighborhood, or what I was about. Some church leaders and a few church planters seemed to understand, yet they found my work unappealing. They were largely uninterested. Something needed to change.

Psalm 16:11 (MSG) says, "Now you've got my feet on the life path, all radiant from the shining of your face. Ever since you took my hand, I'm on the right way." This passage confirmed for me that I was indeed on the right path as I loved my neighbors and committed to my parish. Clinging to this promise, I felt confident linking with others across the region. I began to connect with like-hearted people from around my city.

I formed a team. We compiled a list of people with a reputation for wanting to see transformation in their neighborhoods. Then we reached out. We texted and emailed and used social media. Over dozens of cups of coffee during the next year, I connected with a growing number of lead-ers across my city. My pitch was always the same: "I'd love to hear more about what God is doing in your neighborhood."

That year, I made many new friends, friends who inspire me. Then my team began to host events. This new network now gathers to share stories and talk about what we see, experience, and are learning in our neighborhoods. By overcoming my isolation, I've helped others overcome theirs. As we continue to build connections around the city, we are weaving a beautiful tapestry of grace.

Faithful presence *that cultivates healthy relationships is a monu-mental task that cries for team and camaraderie in the neighborhood. To sit and share stories, to cry together, to be vulnerable about struggles, to hope together, to really understand one another, these things propel me forward personally. And together, our collective strength in Christ is a force that the gates of hell cannot overpower. Linking with people around the city has provided a sense of togetherness. We share the same hope for our different neighborhoods. We share doubts, lament, fear, and failure. And we also celebrate beauty, hope, and God's goodness as it emerges in the communities where we live.*

Here is my advice: Be rooted in your place deeply. Trust our loving God completely. Link locally and broadly. Our collective work needs you, and you cannot do it alone. God be with you as you set about the work in your neighborhood and your city.

—*James, Portland, Oregon*

Time Together

Group Discussion Questions
led by facilitator

1. Choose one of the following to discuss with each other:

   • Refer to the list you created in week two of the disciples in your community. Take a few minutes to pray for the names on this list. Ask God to open doors for you to connect with some like-hearted Christ-followers.

   • Take a moment to brainstorm. Are you aware of any people outside of your parish who might want to engage in a linking relationship? If so, form a plan to make an initial contact with these folks in the next month to discuss how you might be able to connect with one another in a way that benefits each of you.

2. Reread 1 Kings 19:18 out loud. Individually, rewrite this verse in a way that offers you encouragement in your current context and situation. Be sure to write it from the perspective of God speaking directly to you. Share your verses with one another.

3. Read Acts 10:1-5, 21-35, 44-48. Describe what you learn about Cornelius (see verses 1-2 in particular).

4. Notice verses 24, 27, and 33. What do they teach us about People of Peace?

5. In this passage, God brought the Person of Peace to Peter's attention. In Luke 10, Jesus' disciples were sent in pairs to look for them. Off the top of your heads, can you think of any people in your parish who might possibly be People of Peace?

6. Brainstorm together. How might you encourage one another to actively look for the People of Peace that God has placed in your parish(es)?

Take a few moments to pray that God would reveal some People of Peace in your context. Also pray that you will each have the courage to search for those who might live nearby.

Group Activity
led by facilitator

Take a few moments to pull out your phones and research upcoming public community meetings or gatherings being held in your parish. Here are a few possibilities to explore:

- town hall meetings
- public lectures or gatherings (at a local college or library)
- school board meetings
- association meetings (chamber of commerce, HOA, and the like)
- public planning or zoning meetings
- block parties or community festivals

As a group, pick a meeting to attend together, and take some time now to pray for the event. Ask God to reveal any citizens at the gathering who may be People of Peace. Finally, make arrangements to attend the event.

At the gathering, stay attentive to the Spirit's guidance. Engage with any potential People of Peace after the event, and seek to connect further, as appropriate.

Note: This activity may feel like a high challenge for some, and understandably so. However, we encourage you to step into this experience with a mindset to learn and a willingness to be stretched.

Epilogue

Final Thoughts and Moving Forward

If you can't fly, then run. If you can't run, then walk.
If you can't walk, then crawl, but whatever you do,
you have to keep moving forward.

MARTIN LUTHER KING JR.

Our time together is coming to an end. Over these last weeks, we've discovered together that following Jesus is meant to be rooted in place. We've looked at Scripture and heard from real people who are finding the fullness of life in Christ as they invest in their neighborhoods. We've explored different rhythms and practices that can lead to flourishing relationships. Now we invite you to ask, "Where should we go from here?"

On Your Own

What a journey we have been on! We have covered a lot of ground in our time together. Stephanie and I (Julie) hope that the Spirit has provided you with encouragement along the way as well as any needed nudges to continue to lean into the values of place, community, and the unveiling of the Kingdom of God. We also hope that these weeks of learning and experimenting together have stretched, enriched, and inspired you. But before our time together comes to a close, we'd like to leave you with a few thoughts.

God desires for his Kingdom to come and his will to be done in your neighborhood as it is in heaven, and this dream is massively inclusive and beautiful. As this vision comes to fruition, more and more people will experience deeply connected and restored lives with the Father and with one other. At the same time, every aspect of life, even the formal systems that shape our communities, will encounter a foretaste of the promised city of delight. Every person—regardless of skin color, ethnicity, culture, social standing, or wealth—is welcomed into this dream. And as followers of Christ, it is our privilege to join together and come alongside Jesus as he unveils the reality of his Good News and Kingdom reign in the very places in which we live.

Through the previous nine weeks, our hope has been to introduce principles, share stories, and provide activities that allowed you as a group of believers to more deeply explore the realities of your Kingdom home in your current one. We have emphasized the element of community because we truly believe that if we engage one another with enough humility and love, we, as the body of believers, are better together. Our personal lives become more enriched, as does our witness to our neighbors.

During our time together, we hope that you have gotten to know your place a bit more and that a love for your **parish** has been sparked in your heart. We recognize that each person's context is distinct and that there is no cookie-cutter way to love one's neighbors and neighborhood. That said, we hope that you continue to practice **faithful presence** in your parish so that you can respond well to the Spirit's leading in your unique situation.

At this point, you may be wondering, "Where do we go from here?" You have tried out some key practices of shared spiritual life in the context of your parish, but what's next? There is much freedom in how you choose to move forward, but may we offer you a few suggestions?

Your group is at a crossroads and can decide to (1) Lean In, (2) Learn More, or (3) Let Up. *Leaning In* involves continuing to pursue an *Up*, *In*, and *Out* life as a group. *Learning More* is a commitment to continue meeting together in order to explore another resource that expands on some of the concepts presented here. Finally, *Letting Up* is the decision to stop meeting together. Here is an expansion on each of these possibilities:

Lean In

Living an *Up*, *In*, and *Out* life with believers who live near you is foreign territory to many. We suggest that you consider allowing yourselves six to eight months to practice these relational rhythms with one another in your parish. Decide as a group how frequently your *calculated* times together should occur as well as the focus of these times. Also commit to inviting each other into **casual moments** that will allow you to experience life with one another in a more relaxed setting.

At the end of the six to eight months, use the following questions to evaluate whether you would like to continue to function together as a **Committed Community** or if it is time for the group to come to an end. Be sure to allow for safe and honest communication.

- Has our group grown in love and fellowship with one another in a way that makes us want to continue our relationship on behalf of our parish? In other words, have we "gelled," and if so, in what ways?

- Have we been able to agree on *Out* rhythms? Is there a like-hearted vision? If not, can there be?

- Have we used these months with one another to get to know our place better? In what ways have we leaned into the life of our parish?

- Open up discussion about whether or not the group would like to continue and why.

Learn More

Consider diving into another book together. This will continue to expand your joint life in the neighborhood. One possibility to consider is *Practicing the Way of Jesus: Life Together in the Kingdom of Love* by Mark Scandrette. Other books options are listed in appendix B.

Let Up

Even if this tool provided your group with some helpful learning and tangible experiences, you may already know that it is time for your voyage together to come to an end. There are legitimate reasons why this might be the wisest course of action. What we offered you in the beginning was an invitation to experiment and reimagine the very ordinary space you inhabit. We hope that goal has been achieved, even if this is the end of your particular group's time together.

Though this resource has focused on the concept of Committed Community, we do not wish to convey that living as a Committed Community is the only way to be the salt and light of Christ in the places in which we live. Just as you can take a bus, train, or plane to travel across the country, Committed Communities are one vehicle that allow followers of Christ to live life to the full in their parishes.

We believe that this is an effective vehicle worthy of your consideration, and we hope that this tool has expressed that belief. Still, we understand that a Committed Community may not be the best vehicle for you at this time. Whatever the reason, *you are not failing* if you choose not to live as a Committed Community. No matter where you might find yourselves at the end of these ten weeks, all we ask is that you continue to press into the Spirit's leading as it relates to what we've explored.

With the above thoughts in your mind and before your group meets again, please come prepared, having done the following:

- Reflect on Lean In, Learn More, or Let Up. Ask the Lord what he might desire for you and the group with whom you have been gathering. Come ready to discuss which option, in your opinion, seems the most appropriate and why.

- Think through your biggest takeaways from the past nine weeks. Be ready to share one or two things that have encouraged and/or challenged you in a positive way.

Your group facilitator will help to guide this conversation when you are together again. (Facilitator, see appendix A to prepare for this time.) Regardless of what your group decides, we encourage you to end this tenth week on a celebratory note. Enjoy what God has done in and through each of you as individuals and as a group.

Final Thoughts

Whether or not your group disbands, we strongly encourage each of you to seek out at least a few others who might spur you on as you seek to love your neighbors. Again, if you find yourself in need of support, please get in touch with The Navigators Neighbors ministry or The Parish Collective. Contact information can be found in appendix B.

For those who do decide to journey forward together, please know that there is no one set way to function as a group. Some Committed Communities have loose structures that tie them together; others, over time, write up formal covenants to help solidify their identity. Some attend a local, weekly church service; others do not. In our opinion, variety is to be expected, welcomed, and celebrated.

However your group takes shape, we do suggest that you have a person or two whose role it is to guide, vision cast, and help your Committed Community continue to move forward. Having at least one person in this role will keep the group on the same page and assist with details and coordination that will inevitably arise along the way.

Finally, Committed Communities naturally change over time. There are periods of growth, periods of pruning, and even times when they come to an end altogether. In many ways, these types of communities are like living organisms. Though it is tempting to say that groups rooted in place should look and function like x, y, or z, we purposefully tried to keep principles and practices broad enough so that everyone can get in the game. Still, we realize that structure can be helpful. Again we refer you to The Navigators Neighbors and The Parish Collective contact information. Through these resources, you can ask about connecting with current

Committed Communities in order to learn from the variety of expressions that exist around the country.

The title of this resource is *Finding Home*. Indeed, all of creation is longing for its true home with the author and creator of life. But until we are abiding face-to-face with our Lord, Jesus wants to show us the realities of our heavenly home through the overtly divine and painfully ordinary in our very neighborhoods. As disciples seek to come together on behalf of their place in the name of Christ, God's dream of love, restoration, wholeness, and proper worship of his Son will pierce and infuse the people and places around us. We urge you: Continue to dream God's dream with him, for in the end, it is no dream at all but a reality just waiting to happen.

Appendix A

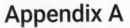

Notes for Facilitators

Notes for Each Session

A good basic structure for each session includes the following:

- check in with everyone to see how they are;
- start with a brief prayer;
- discuss any thoughts on the reading or Bible study;
- do the assigned activity; and
- pray to close.

Some sessions will include watching a video together; there may be additional materials needed for the session, or other ways you might want to prepare in advance. Be sure to review each session closely ahead of the gathering so you feel fully confident as the facilitator.

Notes for the First Session

Week one is designed to help orient people to the study and provide a bit of a road map for what is to come. Some people using this resource will already have a relationship with the other group members. Others might find themselves among those who have a common desire to love their neighbors but have little to no relational history with the rest of the group. If not everyone in the group knows each other, then your first gathering should be spent getting acquainted with one another so that you can experience the benefit of some relational context before digging into the content.

Below is a template for how your first gathering should go. If group members already know each other, then share a meal together and jump to Step 3.

Step 1: Have everyone introduce themselves by giving their name, where they live, and how long they have lived there.

Step 2: Inform the group that the purpose of this gathering is simply to get to know one another. You will be playing a couple of icebreaker games (see below for a few ideas, but feel free to use your own) and then learning about *Finding Home*.

Step 3: After icebreaker games, ask everyone to share their favorite thing about living in their neighborhood and why they said yes to joining this group.

Step 4: Explain details about the *Finding Home* resource as well as any expectations that you have in order for the group to be a good experience for everyone. Examples might include being on time, coming prepared and ready to talk, and being willing to be stretched outside of their comfort zone. Finally, see if anyone has any questions.

Step 5: Make sure everyone is clear on what they need to do before the next meeting. This involves the section marked *On Your Own* in week one. Finally, close the time in prayer (do not ask others to pray out loud at this first gathering).

Icebreaker Ideas

TWO TRUTHS AND A LIE

Have everyone share three interesting facts about themselves. Two of them should be true and one of them a lie. Have everyone guess which one they think is made up.

SENTENCE STARTERS

Print off a paper full of sentence starters for each individual in the group. Give everyone a few minutes to complete the sentences and then go around and share what each person wrote. Sentence starter ideas might include the following:

1. I am . . .
2. I have never . . .
3. I love it when . . .
4. I think I have the best . . .
5. I would never . . .

6. The most important decision I ever made in my life was . . .
7. My happy place is . . .
8. The thing that makes me laugh is . . .
9. There is nothing I enjoy more than . . .
10. I am really good at . . .

THINK FAST

Ask each person to write down ten adjectives about himself or herself in thirty seconds. Go around the room and read them aloud, rapid-fire.

Notes for the Last Session

This final week is an opportunity to make decisions about where to go from here as well as reflect on all that the group has experienced together in the previous weeks. It is a vital week that should not be skipped.

When discussing whether to Lean In, Learn More, or Let Up, it is important to make sure each person gets to voice their opinion or preference. You may find that your group easily comes to a consensus. If so, then great! However, group participants may find themselves divided, and that's okay. Allow for people to disagree with one another over what's next.

If the majority of the group wants to continue together, then those people should set a date on the calendar to talk out specifics of what is ahead. If a smaller portion of the group decides not to continue on, be sure to affirm those individuals. Share with them in what ways you have appreciated having them in the group, and do your best to send them off on a positive note.

Regardless of what everyone decides, end your time looking back. Have each participant share highlights of the previous nine weeks, and allow space to praise God for any work he has done in and through your lives. Also, make a point to voice your own reflections on what you have most appreciated about the journey and the people with whom you have made that journey. Finally, end the night by personally praying for the group.

Thank you for serving each participant as the facilitator. Well done, and may God bless you so that you can richly bless others in return.

Appendix B

Resources for Continued Learning

Connections and Coaches

- The Parish Collective—https://www.parishcollective .org—has excellent resources and ways of connecting you with others around North America and the world who are learning about being practitioners in their neighborhoods.

- The Navigators Neighbors mission—https://neighbors .navigators.org/neighborhood/—offers great resources and coaches who can visit you to offer encouragement and assistance.

Prayer Tools

- "Thirty Days of Praying through Your Neighborhood"— following appendix, also at https://neighbors.navigators .org/neighborhood/

- *The Pray! Prayer Journal*—Dean Ridings

Books

The New Parish—Paul Sparks, Tim Soerens, Dwight
Friesen

Surprise the World—Michael Frost

The Ministry of Ordinary Places—Shannan Martin

The Turquoise Table—Kristin Schell

Thin Places—Jon Huckins, Rob Yackley

To Alter Your World—Michael Frost and Christiana Rice

Living into Community—Christine D. Pohl

Staying Is the New Going—Alan Briggs

Missional: Joining God in the Neighborhood—
Alan J. Roxburgh

The Art of Neighboring—Jay Pathak and Dave Runyon

How to Love Your Neighbor—Amy Lively

Next Door as It Is in Heaven—Lance Ford and
Brad Brisco

Leading Missional Communities—Mike Breen and
the 3DM Team

The Tangible Kingdom—Hugh Halter and Matt Smay

The Intentional Christian Community Handbook—
David Janzen

Slow Church—C. Christopher Smith and John Pattison

Toxic Charity—Robert D. Lupton

Unfettered Hope—Marva J. Dawn

Making Room for Leadership—MaryKate Morse

The Wisdom of Stability—Jonathan Wilson-Hartgrove

Everywhere You Look—Tim Soerens

Practicing the Way of Jesus: Life Together in the Kingdom of Love—Mark Scandrette

Organizations

- The Navigators Neighbors—https://neighbors.navigators .org/neighborhood/

- Parish Collective—https://www.parishcollective.org

- 3DM—https://weare3dm.com

- Thresholds—https://www.thresholdscommunity.org

Appendix C

Thirty Days of Praying through Your Neighborhood

Created by Kirk Lauckner

This is an invitation to audacity—to believe that the gospel is transformative today and that God's Spirit is at work in the uniqueness of our own individuality and that of our neighborhoods.

The Value of a Prayer Walk

Being new to our city, one of the most formational practices that has become a part of my weekly rhythm is to simply walk and pray through my neighborhood. There is something deep and transformational that happens when we walk the streets of our community while conversing with God. I would like to invite you to make a thirty-day "practice" by walking and praying through your own neighborhood.

Day One: WALK. PRAY. PAY ATTENTION. LISTEN.

Lord, would you please deepen my love for my neighborhood, this "place" I call home.

"The Word became flesh and blood, and moved into the neighborhood" (John 1:14, MSG).

Day Two: WALK. PRAY. PAY ATTENTION. LISTEN.

Do I know the names of my neighbors? Lord, help me to learn the names of those living by me.

Day Three: WALK. PRAY. PAY ATTENTION. LISTEN.

Lord, thank you for the gift of a new day! May you surprise me as I walk these streets and enjoy this time with you. May a "divine appointment" happen today!

Day Four: WALK. PRAY. PAY ATTENTION. LISTEN.

When was the last time I was invited into my neighbors' home? When was the last time I had a neighbor over for dinner? Lord, would you give me the time and capacity to practice hospitality? Is there someone we could invite for dinner within the next month?

Day Five: WALK. PRAY. PAY ATTENTION. LISTEN.

Lord, help me to be faithfully present in my neighborhood. May I intentionally say "yes" and "no" to the right things so I have more time for my neighbors.

Day Six: WALK. PRAY. PAY ATTENTION. LISTEN.

What promises am I praying over for my neighborhood? Lord, while I am walking today, please bring to mind specific

Scripture that speaks to loving people, the neighborhood, and the expansion of the gospel.

Day Seven: WALK. PRAY. PAY ATTENTION. LISTEN.

Are there other Christ-followers in my neighborhood? Who else can join us?

Lord, would you please help me identify "People of Peace," or people who care deeply about my neighborhood?

Day Eight: WALK. PRAY. PAY ATTENTION. LISTEN.

Lord, would you please deepen my love for my neighborhood, this "place" I call home?

"The Word became flesh and blood, and moved into the neighborhood" (John 1:14, MSG).

Day Nine: WALK. PRAY. PAY ATTENTION. LISTEN.

Lord, help me to see my neighborhood with your eyes. May my heart break for those things that break your heart.

Day Ten: WALK. PRAY. PAY ATTENTION. LISTEN.

Today while walking, I will bring along a bag and pick up trash along the way.

Lord, thank you for your creation; help me to steward and care for the beauty of the earth you have made.

Day Eleven: WALK. PRAY. PAY ATTENTION. LISTEN.

Today I will give thanks! As I walk, I will focus on the blessings that God has given me. Much like a river that is overflowing, I will allow thanks to well up inside my heart.

Lord, thank you for my neighborhood, my home, food, and the daily comforts that I so often take for granted. Thank you! "So then, just as you received Christ Jesus as Lord, continue to live your lives in him, rooted and built up in him, strengthened in the faith as you were taught, and overflowing with thankfulness" (Colossians 2:6-7).

Day Twelve: WALK. PRAY. PAY ATTENTION. LISTEN.

Today as I walk, I will pay attention to the buildings, the businesses, nonprofits, schools, and churches. What is already happening in my neighborhood, and how may I join in and help these organizations?

Lord, please lead me as I consider how I should become involved in my neighborhood.

Day Thirteen: WALK. PRAY. PAY ATTENTION. LISTEN.

Today I will pray at a park or playground. When was the last time I intentionally visited our community center?

Lord, I long to be a "known character," one who is recognized, loved, and respected. Use me in this "place."

Day Fourteen: WALK. PRAY. PAY ATTENTION. LISTEN.

Today I will pray for laborers to flow out of the neighborhood.

"When he saw the crowds, he had compassion on them, because they were harassed and helpless, like sheep without a shepherd. Then he said to his disciples, 'The harvest is plentiful but the workers are few. Ask the Lord of the harvest, therefore, to send out workers into his harvest field'" (Matthew 9:36-38).

Day Fifteen: WALK. PRAY. PAY ATTENTION. LISTEN.

Lord, would you please deepen my love for my neighborhood, this "place" I call home.

"The Word became flesh and blood, and moved into the neighborhood" (John 1:14, MSG).

Day Sixteen: WALK. PRAY. PAY ATTENTION. LISTEN.

Today I will meditate on these four words: *soften*, *center*, *listen*, and *respond*. Lord, may you keep my heart soft and open, centered in Christ, listening to your Holy Spirit, and responding in love.

Day Seventeen: WALK. PRAY. PAY ATTENTION. LISTEN.

Today I will invite a friend to join me as I walk. (The relationship with this person will determine whether we pray together or simply walk while praying silently.)

"For where two or three gather in my name, there am I with them" (Matthew 18:20).

Day Eighteen: WALK. PRAY. PAY ATTENTION. LISTEN.

"For the whole law can be summed up in this one command: 'Love your neighbor as yourself'" (Galatians 5:14, NLT).

Day Nineteen: WALK. PRAY. PAY ATTENTION. LISTEN.

Which neighbor is God moving and drawing me toward, nudging me to take that next step from acquaintance into relationship?

Lord, will you help me move toward friendship with my neighbors, going beyond simply knowing their names?

Day Twenty: WALK. PRAY. PAY ATTENTION. LISTEN.

"You are the light of the world. A town built on a hill cannot be hidden. Neither do people light a lamp and put it under a bowl. Instead they put it on its stand, and it gives light to everyone in the house. In the same way, let your light shine before others, that they may see your good deeds and glorify your Father in heaven" (Matthew 5:14-16).

Day Twenty-One: WALK. PRAY. PAY ATTENTION. LISTEN.

When was the last time we had a party at our house? Who could we invite? Who could help us? "Then Levi held a great banquet for Jesus at his house, and a large crowd of tax collectors and others were eating with them" (Luke 5:29).

Day Twenty-Two: WALK. PRAY. PAY ATTENTION. LISTEN.

Lord, thank you for the gift of a new day! May you surprise me as I walk these streets and enjoy this time with you. May a "divine appointment" happen today!

Day Twenty-Three: WALK. PRAY. PAY ATTENTION. LISTEN.

Lord, would you please deepen my love for my neighborhood, this "place" I call home?

"The Word became flesh and blood, and moved into the neighborhood" (John 1:14, MSG).

Day Twenty-Four: WALK. PRAY. PAY ATTENTION. LISTEN.

Today as I walk, I will ask God to give me a picture of what our neighborhood could become.

Lord, please increase the vision for my neighborhood.

Day Twenty-Five: WALK. PRAY. PAY ATTENTION. LISTEN.

Today as I walk, I will pray for insight on how I can "**link**" with other neighborhoods within my city.

Day Twenty-Six: WALK. PRAY. PAY ATTENTION. LISTEN.

"The number-one obstacle to neighboring well is time. . . . Do you currently live at a pace that allows you to be present in your neighborhood?"[1]

Day Twenty-Seven: WALK. PRAY. PAY ATTENTION. LISTEN.

"From one man he made all the nations, that they should inhabit the whole earth; and he marked out their appointed times in history and the boundaries of their lands" (Acts 17:26).

Day Twenty-Eight: WALK. PRAY. PAY ATTENTION. LISTEN.

"Remember that God is and has been at work in your neighborhood. Part of leading is attuning yourself to the breath of God bringing new life to the dry bones of your place. Live in the freedom that comes from knowing that God loves your neighborhood far more than you ever will. You actually can trust God's love for your place."[2]

Day Twenty-Nine: WALK. PRAY. PAY ATTENTION. LISTEN.

Lord, would you please deepen my love for my neighborhood, this "place" I call home?

"The Word became flesh and blood, and moved into the neighborhood" (John 1:14, MSG).

Day Thirty: WALK. PRAY. PAY ATTENTION. LISTEN.

"I'll be with you as you do this, day after day after day, right up to the end of the age" (Matthew 28:20, MSG).

*   *   *

Thank you for taking the time to WALK. PRAY. PAY ATTENTION. LISTEN. I hope this will stimulate a lifetime practice of prayer for the place where you live. Whether you reside in the heart of a major city, in suburbia, or in the middle of the countryside, God has people who live right where you are. I can't wait to see what God will do in your neighborhood! Love deeply, and give your life away for the sake of the Kingdom!

Notes

GLOSSARY OF TERMS

1. Paul Sparks, Tim Soerens, and Dwight J. Friesen, *The New Parish: How Neighborhood Churches Are Transforming Mission, Discipleship and Community* (Downers Grove, IL: IVP Books, 2014), 23.
2. Project for Public Spaces, "Ray Oldenburg," December 31, 2008, https://www.pps.org/article/roldenburg. Oldenburg coined the term *third places.*

WEEK TWO: COMMITTED COMMUNITY

1. Lisa Sharon Harper, *The Very Good Gospel: How Everything Wrong Can Be Made Right* (Colorado Springs: WaterBrook, 2016), 30–32.
2. Brené Brown, "America's Crisis of Disconnection Runs Deeper than Politics," *Fast Company*, September 12, 2017, https://www.fastcompany.com/40465644/brene-brown-americas-crisis-of-disconnection-runs-deeper-than-politics.
3. TEDx Talks, "The Lethality of Loneliness: John Cacioppo at TEDxDesMoines," YouTube video, September 9, 2013, https://www.youtube.com/watch?v=_0hxl03JoA0.

WEEK THREE: WHY PLACE MATTERS

1. Mark Twain, *Tales, Speeches, Essays, and Sketches* (New York: Penguin, 1994), 361.
2. According to *The International Standard Bible Encyclopedia*, Decapolis is "the name given to the region occupied by a league of 'ten cities.'" The cities were not Jewish but Greek. *International Standard Bible Encyclopedia* (1915), s.v. "Decapolis."

3. Paul Sparks, Tim Soerens, and Dwight J. Friesen, *The New Parish: How Neighborhood Churches Are Transforming Mission, Discipleship and Community* (Downers Grove, IL: IVP Books, 2014), 23.

WEEK FOUR: FAITHFUL PRESENCE IN THE PARISH

1. These ideas are based on concepts discussed by Paul Sparks, Tim Soerens, and Dwight Friesen in *The New Parish: How Neighborhood Churches Are Transforming Mission, Discipleship and Community* (Downers Grove, IL: IVP Books, 2014).
2. Nicholas Wolterstorff, *Until Justice and Peace Embrace* (Grand Rapids, MI: Eerdmans, 1987), 140.
3. Observations on the boundaries of Israel originated with biblical scholar David Shive.

WEEK FIVE: LIVING UP, IN, AND OUT

1. Mike Breen and Steve Cockram, *Building a Discipling Culture: How to Release a Missional Movement by Discipling People Like Jesus Did*, 2nd ed. (Pawleys Island, SC: 3 Dimension Ministries, 2011), 80.

WEEK SIX: MOVING UP

1. Aaron Niequist, *The Eternal Current: How a Practice-Based Faith Can Save Us from Drowning* (Colorado Springs: Waterbrook, 2018), 14.
2. For the lyrics and history of this liturgy, see https://www.anewliturgy.com /no-6-.

WEEK SEVEN: MOVING IN

1. We are grateful to Lorae Kinseth of The Navigators for editing this story.

WEEK EIGHT: MOVING OUT

1. Blue Letter Bible, "Lexicon: Strong's G965—*bēthleem*," accessed November 19, 2020, https://www.blueletterbible.org/lang/lexicon/lexicon .cfm?Strongs=G965&t=NIV.

WEEK NINE: THE POWER OF LINKING

1. Paul Sparks, Tim Soerens, and Dwight Friesen, *The New Parish: How Neighborhood Churches Are Transforming Mission, Discipleship and Community* (Downers Grove, IL: IVP Books, 2014), 32.
2. Ideas in this chapter are based on concepts discussed by Tim Soerens in his book *Everywhere You Look: Discovering the Church Right Where You Are* (Downers Grove, IL: InterVarsity Press, 2020).

3. Helena Williams, "Six Facts about Elephant Families," *The Independent*, December 19, 2013, https://www.independent.co.uk/voices/comment/six -facts-about-elephant-families-9015298.html.

APPENDIX C: THIRTY DAYS OF PRAYING THROUGH YOUR NEIGHBORHOOD

1. Jay Pathak and Dave Runyon, *The Art of Neighboring: Building Genuine Relationships Right Outside Your Door* (Grand Rapids, MI: Baker Books, 2012), 43, 189.
2. Paul Sparks, Tim Soerens, and Dwight J. Friesen, *The New Parish: How Neighborhood Churches Are Transforming Mission, Discipleship, and Community* (Downers Grove, IL: IVP Books, 2014), 183.